CW00433934

16 ROOMS

AND THE USE OF THE

BLACKHOUSES

ADVANCED

DIRECTIONAL

SORCERY

BY

SORCERESS CAGLIASTRO

IRON RING PUBLISHING
COPYRIGHT 2016

DEDICATION

To the labyrinth that is

9

WARNING

DO NOT SHARE THIS BOOK.
PLACE YOUR BLOOD IN THIS CIRCLE.

THIS IS BLOOD SORCERY........

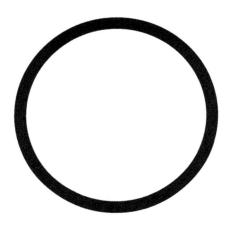

NOTE – READ INSTRUCTIONS
CAREFULLY AND THOROUGHLY PRIOR
TO PERFORMING THE SORCERY
HEREIN ... S9

TABLE OF CONTENTS

PERSONAL FORWARD

This is a transcript of a series of classes on Polarities of Polarities, in other words, in the expansion of Directional Sorcery to offer sixteen additional and more focused options to utilize within Directional Sorcery as well as a series of classes addressing the use of BLACKHOUSES.

Since offering these classes students have utilized these rooms and the BLACKHOUSES extensively and are finding great success utilizing this more profound and specific focus.

Remember that this book is based on transcripts. It is meant to feel that way – as if the reader is participating. All of the work comes from observation, discussions with Daemons and testing resulting in reliable data – and is offered once it is established that this aspect of the work is now a process that delivers...

I have been a Sorceress since birth. I don't say that in the way that girls with newly dyed black hair and Alchemy pendants suddenly notice that their grandmothers were witches.... I make my claim on much more profoundly provable references as well as the facts... The facts..... I rarely use that word. To expand on that indulge me while I mention the following data.... I have spent (used, lived...spent) most of my life studying, building and perfecting this work as if the energies that be, kept all the other options for a career or life just out of reach. Sorcery has been the schoolmarm who has wrapped my knuckles whenever my hand reached for a prize other than this one. Anytime my outstretched hand filled out an application for a graduate program in neuroscience, or agreed to travel to pursue a profound education in archaic languages the ruler hit my hand and she said – leave that to the "archaics" those enamored only by that which is old and already told.... You Miss, will crawl around in cemeteries and find a way for the inhabitants to talk to you – clearly – and then when you do you will teach it to others.   Once that is done you will sit alone in the dark for days, weeks, months at a time until the Pillars come to you and they will make sense – and then you will teach   them   to   others.

The schoolmarm in this narrative is a ten foot Daemon known only as 9........and he and he alone pulls me back to center when I think I will have instead a little shop filled with pretty dresses, perform Sorcery alone and leave my books to do the teaching.... 9, my darling 9 says no to that.... taking and giving I suppose....however as long as I agree to never stop developing and teaching the work, a side passion of professional poker is not off the table – a play on words...yes...

9.... you are alright...

My books are larger print so they are more visually accessible, as well as formatted with generous room to write ...as my audience tends to dislike bright lights...

Write in this book....drip all over it...after all – it belongs to you.....

Sorceress Cagliastro, Blood Sorceress, Necromancer in the hands of 9

A brief review......

NORTH – BRINGS CONNECTON

SOUTH – BREAKS BONDS

EAST – SPEEDS ACTION UP

WEST – APPROPRIATE TIMING.

If you are not familiar with the basics, go back and read

EITHER OR BOTH of the following books:

+BLOOD SORCERY BIBLE VOL II – STRIKING THE TARGET, the Practitioner and the Static Practice

+THE SCIENCE OF SORCERY

BEGINNER COURSE VOLUME 1,

BLOOD SORCERY AND DIRECTIONAL SORCERY TRANSCRIPTS

STARTING POINT....

WEDNESDAY NIGHT

CORE CLASS

TRANSCRIPT

POLARITIES OF POLARITIES

I am going to jump right in with this, because this is a complex ritual/procedural experience, whichever language you prefer. Once I found it to be the right time to share this information, I discussed this with some of my Attending Daemons, and we talked about how the polarities affect the Daemons, and whether or not they are comfortable in terms of our recognition and thereby usage of the polarities. So I did an experiment with them in the Static Practice,... and how to language and tach this advanced work, and it came to me in that experiment...perhaps I will talk a little

about that as we go on....
In that experiment, they, my Attending Daemons, were able to work with the polarities, when they are given directions, or when negotiations were made, or whatever it is that was best to do when they are off to do something on my behalf. Yes it is a negotiation when we adhere to what we understand the properties of the Four Polarities to be.

However they are richer than that in their understanding, and they are richer than we are in our understanding, because they are just energy. They are an amalgam of chaos.

They are a ball of some sort of pseudo-magnetic dust.

So they are living in a truth regarding the polarities that **our** constant cognitive experience interrupts, and our own requirement to participates thereby precludes us from a front seat to the obvious....such is the human/Daemon relationship....

What to do.....

So I looked at it, and what they get out of the polarities. The data shows that it's like MapQuest to them. Use of the Polarities in our communications delivers clearer directives to them. So I did a thing where I went into the Static Practice, which is most of the time anyway, but I very specifically went into the Static Practice, **and I went into each of the polarities and was told that inside the polarities, the aspects of the other polarities can rule**... and if not fully rule, fine tune the polarity itself. So first let me just say anecdotally, if one found oneself in a room called the North, **within** the North, one could focus North,

South, East, or West. So there is a second level of pure clarity that the Daemons go through in terms of their response to the magnetic aspects of the polarity.

To be clear this work, these 16 Rooms and the BLACKHOUSES is broad – not only for use with Daemons…

So I've been doing this work for a long time and recently I decided that I would give Daemons directives only in this capacity, which for them, in some ways is stepping backwards because there's no language, yet they were willing to participate.

I used two of my Attending Daemons, and Pitcher John, and I made that choice because my Attending Daemons are logical and clear, and were doubly engaged as they took an interest in also focusing on Pitcher John as he is a wild man, so I wanted to see what the difference in their temperament would bring to the outcome. Remember, with Daemons, temperament is so important. For example, if you're working with the JACK558, the canine Daemon, (from 26 Daemons Revisited) and you have a pretty clear focus, you know that this Daemon is probably not going to rip your face off. On the flipside then you go and work with NOHG (also a Daemon from the book 26 Daemons Revisited, available on amazon.com/author/sorceresscagliastro), or one of the warriors, or this kind of thing, or you work with your own Attending Daemons, there's all kinds of madness that can go on because of their temperament which so clearly defines who they are. Because they have this experience where they are built from a process, and in the process they become fully what they are, they are genuine throughout.....

You know the question of nature and nurture? It's all nature with Daemons. They come from a certain type of chaos, they are a certain type of chaos, and they deliver their work in a certain way related to that chaos. They don't go through a lot of learning to be different than the way they are, because it is not natural for them to do so, because they are an amalgam of magnetic dust, with some kind of consciousness.

So what we're talking about tonight is new to this advanced class. Just the way the Fifth Pillar (not yet available to the public) was a new thing which I hadn't yet taught, broadly, only some of the students attending tonight have heard about it.

16 ROOMS and BLACKHOUSS are new opportunities in terms of what advanced students can do in their process of controlling their Attending Daemons and so much more as **all of this new information is useful when NEGOTIATING with Daemons.** Now let me give you a little understanding about where this group is with Attending Daemons. Almost all of you (TO STUDENTS) have made some kind of reliable contact.

Allow me to define; **reliable contact** means

+you've seen the same thing more than twice

+you've been able to bring or lead that which you have contacted to a place, say your living room for example....

+You've had a conscious experience with that entity where you feel the same way each time

+You're not living in trepidation regarding the entity

+You have some understanding that this is a different entity than one that might be sent to you in a hostile act by someone else.

Some of you have much more profound relationships than that, but that is really the baseline as to what's necessary to be sure that we are dealing with Attending Daemons.

So now that information is sort of in place in a way, what we're looking at now is this - can we start to direct them, and make them act on our behalf, and this is necessary because it's like a mob family, something I understand well, so I speak from it. People come into it to work with the group, and then they have to pass some kind of test in which they test themselves. Tests can be many things, with humans. It can be loyalty, with animals as we can see their emotional IQ, if they are going to attack you, etc. However with Daemons, it's really sort of an arch addressing the question - Do they really understand what I'm saying to them? Am I plugging this in in the right place? I've started to address these scenarios by stripping apart the big story called - go make a deal with your Attending Daemons. That is what I say, and now I'm breaking it down into tiny little pieces, not because you can't do it, but because you finally can.

So now there are going to be tiny little pieces, by which I mean; and I like this term, tiny little pieces for this project, or process, and we're going to do this for at least two weeks, and these tiny little pieces are exemplified as follows –

Example ...you go in through the north, and in the north, the thing that is now being attached to you, or being increased, shouldn't come at you like a speeding train. There should be a mechanism for you to be able to control its speed, its impact, its duration, and when it gets there. So inside the polarities, we are going to use all of the other polarities in each room to explore and utilize their nuances and blatant strengths.

If you look at what's on my screen,

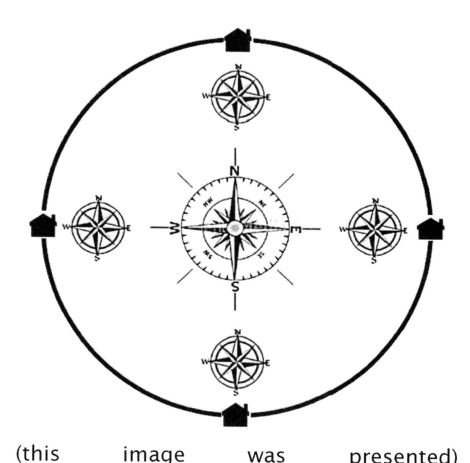

(this image was presented)

This is quite simply a compass built from five compasses, presenting the North, South, East and West aspects within the original four polarities, and the

BLACKHOUSES (Part Two of this book), are represented. So for example if we are in the north, we can look at the east aspect of the North, the south aspect of the north, the west aspect of the north, and the pure north aspect of the north. The last one is known as one of the Double Labeled Rooms (which you will be addressing in the section discussing the BLACKHOUSES)..I am going this route because this seems to be how the Daemons navigate and how much gets done in Directional Sorcery....

I said to 9, I desire for this thing (ANY

PERSONAL EXAMPLE) to happen... I require this thing to happen, and I require this to happen so that the person it's happening to is going to get the most out of it. In one example, the person to which this is happening had a requirement to maintain a connection to employment over a period of time. So we went north, and I looked at that, and I said to 9, go shake those people up, and get them on the phone and make that thing happen. Then 9 noticed it was the middle of the night. I asked what this meant to him? He said it does not fit with the regular activity. **He** had observed that people don't get phone calls for jobs at 3:00 in the morning. So we had to continue the connection of placing the work "as if it has already happened", so we worked in the north, staying with a position called 'it already happened'. At that point we **bent** it west so there was appropriate timing, allowing the work to land where it needed to land the next day. This is not the same as the splits of the polarities (ne, sw etc), this is **bending**, putting the arrow in the bow, pulling it, and making sure that arrow not only is it going to the target, but it's either sharp enough to kill, or dull enough not to kill, or it's got a suction cup on the end because a toddler's using it. It must have that level of specificity and honing when you're shooting the thing, so that it lands exactly and appropriately.

A long story to outline an example of using two opposing polarities follows...(remember this is a transcript). This was something I was not expecting to talk about this soon, after working on it with 9, and 2, and 5, who is **extremely** determined to add his input into the story all the time. There is a term that my daughter and I use, which reminds me of my Attending Daemon 5. We didn't invent it, but we use it occasionally as it comes from my background The term is **mob wife**. A mob wife is someone who benefits from all the activity, yet doesn't have to participate in any of the activity, rather, just keeping quiet. 5 is much like a mob wife. 5 will go take all the benefits of becoming more tangible and getting better and stronger, and being able to do all of that he can do now, and not really giving credit to those who provide these opportunities. This is his way.

I don't talk about 5 often, so when working with him one must understand his proclivity toward self-aggrandizement. **So when I'm working with him, I have to make him feel like he's appreciated and present the work so that he feels some kind of pleasure.** Then when I ask him to go do something expeditiously, I work towards the East because Daemons work so well in polarities, I have to remember that he has to be **efficient** as well at the task, which means that I will take a little bit of the West – an aspect or two, to facilitate his completion of the task. However East/West is not a split, it is a method of utilizing **both** polarities as contributors to the Sorcery event.

So we are talking about going into the 'individual rooms', yet remembering to consider the main energy – the main polarity – so that the four individual rooms benefit from being a four room suite. So in the Northern Polarity, there are four rooms, Northern Polarity East Room, Northern Polarity South Room, Northern Polarity West Room and the DOUBLE LABELED one – Northern Polarity North Room. Start with any polarity and list the rooms going clockwise from the one past the original polarity.

That method assures us that when we return to the fourth room, it is the pure room, the Double Labeled Room associated with the particular polarity.

To provide further clarity, the language is also, when, staying with the same example of the North, and utilizing the east room, the phase the <u>Eastern Aspect of the North/Northern Polarity</u> is another way that may be phrased.

Now that I have said all of that, think for a second about the gallery in the Static Practice, because when you're in the Static Practice you have your gallery of everything that's gone on; everything you've ever experienced. Yet what you don't have the best access to in the gallery is that of which you are **unaware** of having experienced because the gallery in the Static Practice is a very visual place, and tends toward showing that which you will readily recognize. There is an upside to that. If going through massive life changes or trauma, as it is for someone who feels their life looks very different than it did yesterday, it may be best not to be confronted with seeing everything in the gallery at once. In that circumstance, seeing what today looks like, and not being asked to compare it to yesterday may be quite appreciated. The Gallery in the Static Practice is good to its human...

Just as we have the opportunity to look at polarities through the nuances of the rooms within them, we can also look at the Static Practice through the nuances of the collection in the Gallery. For example if on the wall in your gallery there is a tableau of your college graduation, when looking at it you know that you did X amount of work, and received your degree etc... However that image in your gallery is not likely to bring about broader or unrelated memories. It is a snapshot of a particular nuance of an event (going to college) that is quite significant, yet no broader thoughts are brought through this image. This assists the human mind in editing out small slivers of nuances when building a Sorcery event from the Static Practice gallery.

In the 16 rooms, we are looking at the rooms within the polarity. We are going to go through them logistically in terms of the polarities, and spend a few minutes in each one as I leave them open so you can get the sensation. This is a big task as there are 16 of them. (Readers benefit from having this book as students took extensive notes from the live class). (to live class students) and I am going to ask you to listen to this class again, so that by the next class when we actually work in these 16 rooms, you will have an understanding; a feeling for what it means to be in there.

Let's talk for a minute about triggers. When you are in each of the rooms, it doesn't have to be tonight because you're going to do listen (readers study from the text) before the next class, create some kind of trigger that helps you remember the experience. For example, when you are in the north, and you really have a desire for something to come straight at you in your life, but you don't want to get knocked down by it, create an image that means that so you can revisit it.

Several years ago I had a client who won a lot of money. He said his initial thought was wow I have 5 million dollars now, this is excellent! His whole life came apart. It came at him like a high speed train and he didn't even know what to do with that. By the time he came to me he was already in complete devastation over it, but he said something very interesting. He said; I did not think a train carrying 5 million dollars coming my way could be a bad thing. **I said; well, it's still a train, and it was still barreling at you, therefore the details of the contents are not really significant when a train is doing that.....**

So the question is; when a potential opportunity comes at you that way do you get off the tracks, do you let it hit you and see what happens? Triggers help navigate these experiences in all the pillars, and at the very tactile level in Directional Sorcery. So when we start to talk about something powerful like the Northern Polarity, we are demanding something to come to us in a really proactive way. What one must remember is that there is an opportunity; a second level of opportunity to still control the speed, still control the incoming, and still control the construct of that thing by understanding that even inside of a polarity, there are the other inner rooms... and that's what we're going to talk about moving forward tonight.

I am going to go through all the rooms while accessing them so they are present and you can feel them. I will spend perhaps two minutes in each one so you can have the experience of that, (readers do the exercise anyway). I ask that you think about triggers while doing so. Think about what you FELT as Directional Sorcery is tactile. Be specific. Ask yourself questions which will dig into the moment.

"Did I feel cold? Did I feel vacuous? Did I feel nothing? Did I have a memory of something?" Because when you do this in the Static Practice, which is what I'm going to ask you to do also tonight; to the best of your ability; the Static Practice will start to show you images from your gallery. You may find that this is going to be really eviscerating. Stuff is going to come up...and to be clear you know, this isn't therapy... it's straight ahead physics – straight ahead IRON RING SORCERY.

The principles and study of physics shows us that things are prone to jumping from one connection to another. This is a huge part of the Sorcery I practice. If you **had** a memory that you no longer are clear about, and you really have a requirement to reconnect with that memory, perhaps from some period in your life that you've shut off, the North will give you those memories back. However you most likely do not desire the overwhelm, as if they are pouring into your head one after the next because it was painful enough for you to shut them down to begin with. To control the flow you must have some kind of mechanism, so add the western aspect of the north for appropriate timing, as you still desire forward movement, however you desire for it to be at **your** pace.

Prepare yourself with an understanding that when you're in there, reactions may; even at this very first pass through this thing, where we're just looking at the rooms; appear and it may be a lot to process. Use what comes up as triggers.

Utilize the compass image that I offered earlier, presenting all 16 additional rooms and the 4 originally named.

Let's begin…

I'm going to start with the south, so what you're doing here is creating some kind of an acceptance to broaden your story, your understanding, your interpretation of what the polarities are capable of doing. Here is one more example; I know that some of you are involved in the legal field, so if you're in court and you have someone on the stand, you know that this person has to give evidence, and they have to say, certain things. Yet you have a thought in your mind that if these things are out of order, they will change the outcome. If the jury hears these things, not in your preferred order, but in the preferred order of the person whose speaking, then there could be less of the absolute result than you desire.

So you're sitting there, and you really want to get her to say everything that she needs to say, so you're working in the north. Now you have a sensation that she really wants to talk about the thing she is supposed to say last, or some other out of order situation. So you listen very carefully to your Divination aspect, and it appears that the statement she is about to make is not supposed to be first. You must get her to slow down. Get her to take time to think. The statement that's coming the fastest is not the one you with which she should open. Therefore, you're going to slow that up with the south. If you don't think that she can gather her thoughts together at all, and you think there is going to be a conflict and a jam up, then you stay in the north room in the north polarity to keep the flow going. Once you start to feel it happening, you can start to operate either in the east to speed it up, or the west to handle the pacing, or in the south to slow it down and give her a chance to think, so maybe you can ask the question again.

So you see how important Sorcery is in terms of the everyday experience, even at that kind of professional level. This is really important information. **Here you are learning the opposite of allow, in a way, which is "pause".** At some point over the next few weeks, I'm going to go back to the parts in the 5th pillar (not yet a publically available subject) to go over all of those aspects that we talked about. The importance of what I called "STOP" and other parts of the Fifth Pillar, and bring that back in to this conversation, however not tonight. Just allow yourself to understand tonight that the word **pause** might mean something valuable to you. **The Science of Sorcery is a stop and think path. Stop, Pause,** these are words that will give you a moment to say ok; I'm in the north and I'm in the east now, so I want it to come at me faster, I get it. Or, no, I would like you to **pause** for a moment and have the experience.

So for the purpose of tonight, I'm placing a portal on this class, in which case everything that you do in this work is irrelevant <u>for tonight</u>. <u>It is a safe zone</u>. (readers of the book – when you have the book open and you read those words – you will experience the same safe zone by the action of a principle known as **MIMICRY)**. So nothing changes for you), because if you're going into these rooms usually you want to change something, or you want to create an experience. I have a desire for nothing to get damaged in your world during this process, so I am utilizing the **TEACHING PLATFORM**, which is a safe zone that I use when teaching something that is new to students. I did it with the Fifth Pillar the first time so that you're not adjusting what's going on in your world until this class is over, when you have of course, every right to go work on this on your own in order to acclimate. This is complex work...I find in certain situations it is best to hear the complex version first and settle into the information which follows it with a honed ear. That was the point of this long introduction.

It is advisable that you have the illustration of the multiple compasses with the BLACKHOUSES set in at the ready while this discussion continues. Place it in front of you so that it is in alignment with the actual polarities. We will work clockwise. When learning this work, one can review and study either going counter-clockwise or clockwise as long as one does it all the same all the time. Doing so ALLOWS for a pathway of the knowledge to "sink in" – to coin an often used colloquium.

In this particular exercise of learning to just introduce you to the rooms, I'm going to go clockwise around the polarities (ex:North, East, South, West) as well as within the polarities (ex:North Polarity East room, North Polarity South room, North Polarity West Room, North Polarity North Room).

So we're going to start with the west and what we're going to do first is this; everyone will take minute to get into the Static Practice. I will time it so that we have enough time to do all of them, or at least to go through them all, and I will talk you through what we are going to do.

So if everyone could just find themselves in the Static Practice, and understand that I am working on your behalf to make sure that no changes occur during this experience that would be helpful. Take a minute to do that.

Remember this – we are purely dealing with **what** the polarities do. We are **not** adding subject matter to them, we are **understanding** the presence of the west. West is a polarity which brings us to a place where things are **appropriately timed**. It is usually the most complex of the four; the one that people have the hardest time understanding, because the word "appropriate" is so subjective. **Appropriate means, for our purposes, that the experience occurs in the <u>best paced scenario</u> for the outcome of success in terms of rate of which one can handle receiving.** If you're doing this to receive something that you desire – **the West ALLOWS time for the placement of that desire to come into play so you are fully prepared to receive it.** If you are using Sorcery for example to put someone in distress, then it will happen in the period of time that you require it to happen **for your perfect desired result**. If you are doing this to put something into your life, that you require; a lover, a job, even a fresh perspective, whatever you like, it will come to you in the amount of **paces** that it takes for you to fully grasp it without being damaged or overwhelmed.

To be clear this is not the same as open ended "waiting and wishing"...that is for glitter, pink candles and prayer groups – this is the Science of Sorcery – appropriate pacing SERVES the practitioner, it is not a delay distractor...

TEACHING NOTE

You will see from this class (and readers you will surely see it in this book) **that I will repeat information in long and short forms as this is all new and the student's mind must be given time to "catch up" to this material.**

First, so that there is an opportunity to grasp the language – I will begin with the shorthand version of the Rooms within the Polarities...

BLANK IMAGE TO CLEAR YOUR MIND

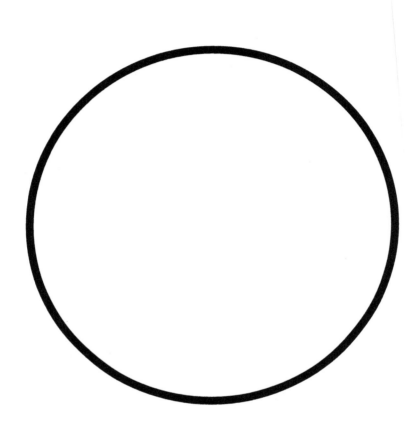

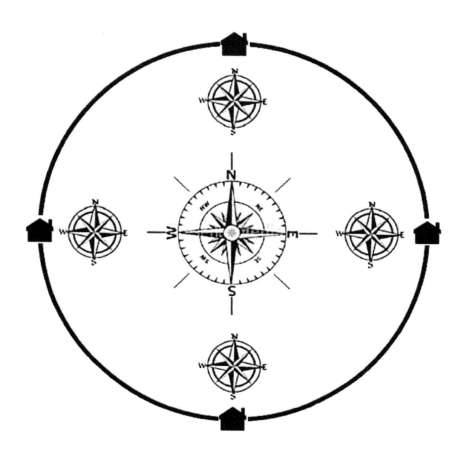

ROOMS WITHIN THE POLARITIES

Each of the four polarities has its own set of Directional Polarities. Allow yourself to think of the main polarity I address each time (for example, the Northern Polarity) as the CENTER of a compass as we are working through all of the polarities individually – and see from that point of view the four directions surrounding that Polarity.

First I will give you the concise version of the ROOMS WITHING THE POLARITIES then move into expanded versions..... Please remember to keep your mind on the main polarity in some way each time as it is the feed to the other four rooms in its "neighborhood"

NORTH POLARITY - EAST ROOM

Being in this room is an opportunity for you to put **someone else's** mind into a constant sensation of waiting. Waiting is a very uncomfortable thing.

In the east room in the north polarity, you can create a sensation of neurosis for someone so they become very high strung, and always scurrying to seek the next opportunity, almost the way someone acts who is seeking out a drug. They are never settled as they are never living in the moment. Use it to distract someone when you require a to take the prize you both seek...

NORTH POLARITY – SOUTH ROOM

This is an "unfriendly" thing to use, it doesn't mean that you can't use it. It gives the individual who you're focused on a sensation of **on-going and profound trepidation** that is relentless. The "other shoe falling".., another rug being pulled out from under them etc.. They start to connect these feelings as a way of life, and this ongoing trepidation creates in a person the sensation of panic. **So if you want to stagger somebody out of something; out of their own opportunity, this is the way to do it.**

<u>NORTH</u> POLARITY – WEST ROOM

We have an opportunity to place a type of desired plateaus; areas of leveling off which is really the delivery of what we're asking to have happen **TO BE CLEAR -** **when I use the word <u>asking</u>, I am not asking for a delivery by any divinity, but rather we are solidifying our own intentions**, the way one places a theory or an experience of experiment inside of the process of setting up a ritual for sorcery. The west will purposefully and appropriately pace the delivery so that it is profound and well absorbed and savored.

NORTH POLARITY – NORTH ROOM

– This is sort of the "nice guy". This is good delivery, solid information, delivered well, delivered strong, full contact. Don't use it unless there is an agreement of delivery here. Something you absolutely desire, something someone else absolutely desires is required here.

Change your polarity association to the EAST now…..

EAST POLARITY – SOUTH ROOM

The connection of the southern room in the eastern polarity is to send a sensation of trepidation or of impending finality. If you are using the southern room in the eastern polarity to create some devastation on someone or on something, they will find themselves in a state of complete trepidation as if knowing it's coming. "Walking the plank"…That's the "talent" of the southern room in the eastern polarity.

EAST POLARITY - WEST ROOM

This **allows you a stop action control mechanism.** Consider this .... **When you let the yo-yo drop, if you will, the return speed is the same as the drop speed. What the west does is, it allows you to insert pauses into the return – controlling the receiving of that which you are creating.** This can be a torturous experience if what you're creating is a conflict within the desire to receive something with immediacy. One can use this on themselves to savor a situation – take caution- because the pauses can embed without removal skills...

EAST POLARITY – NORTH ROOM

This is the ER of the rooms of the polarities. If something must happen right away, and that which must happen right away has a sensation (this is what the data shows) that it is a thing of super-human capacity to handle, then this is your room. Examples - getting out of somewhere that has tremendous danger; stopping the bleeding of someone who is damaged and bleeding out, holding back a child in utero so that the woman does not lose it early....these and other perceived urgencies...

EAST POLARITY – EAST ROOM

It makes something happen so quickly that it distorts time in terms of the receiver. If you are working on something where you have a desire to make someone forget something, the eastern room of the eastern polarity is the way to go. What happens here is that the activity is sped up so quickly that the receiver doesn't perceive it to have happened. This is a sort of **bending** memory. **I strongly suggest that you not use this one upon yourself.**

SOUTH POLARITY - WEST ROOM

This is a room where malice is part of your intention. Utilize this room when you are trying to create a situation where you are separating from something, which is what the south does; breaking a bond between the practitioner and the other individual, the practitioner and a habit, or a subject and a habit, or a subject and another individual. **The western room will allow for there to be a painful exchange in that separation. The painful aspect shows up in the stalled and started pattern of the West - causing disgust and permanent disconnect.**

SOUTH POLARITY – NORTH ROOM

The northern room in the southern polarity allows you to create a manner of second level scenarios where the bond is broken, and the individual with whom it's broken, or the experience with whom it is broken has the sensation that the breaking has occurred. This is not good when you want to hide something, but it's very good when you want to say; **I have separated from you and now you feel it too.**

SOUTH POLARITY – EAST ROOM

This is a highly visceral experience; the eastern room of the south because you are saying that the connection that you have a desire to break must be broken with immediacy; with top speed, as fast as possible. This room works fully on the separation and not on notifying parties. This is **urgent care** not a soap opera...

SOUTH POLARITY – SOUTH ROOM

It causes sort of a fever pitch of breaking - the way one thinks of rubber bands snapping, and buildings falling, and the kind of thing where a breakaway is a powerful tactile experience. This is non emotional and all visceral -much more so than the western aspect as there is **not** a requirement for any kind of malfeasance. **I use this when destroying tumors.**

<u>WEST</u> POLARITY – NORTH ROOM

The room in the north will bring to you a tighter bond, a more powerful connection, so that when the material is delivered it has a higher sticking value. It will stay longer. I phrase it that way because permanence is a complex issue in Sorcery as all that can be done can be undone if one has the appropriate skills.

WEST POLARITY – EAST ROOM

Appropriate timing could benefit by the assistance of a push – the East provides that. The push however is on the recipient not on the timing in and of itself... The recipient benefits (and of course the recipient could be the Practitioner) from an increased capacity to take on the coming events, responses or conclusion. This is a unique room in so much that one applies it to the situation (to the movement) and it is received by the involved individual (the stationary).

<u>WEST</u> POLARITY – SOUTH ROOM

The south will put a greater distance between the process and the target, moving things so they are not able to make full contact. So one has to ask oneself what it would look like to apply appropriate timing to the dissolution of bonds? This is best prescribed for something that must be eased out or someone who must be let out/down gently.

<u>WEST</u> POLARITY – WEST ROOM

When you use the western aspect of the western polarity then what you're doing is committing, allowing, accepting the full actions of the west to deliver in appropriate timing, taking out of this equation; your understanding of what appropriate timing might be in this situation. Here you are allowing for pure physics to make that delivery. Advanced skills are not necessary – **however once done, without advanced skills of reversal this process is in full bind....**

This image is here for repositioning the self back to center...focus on the black center dot..

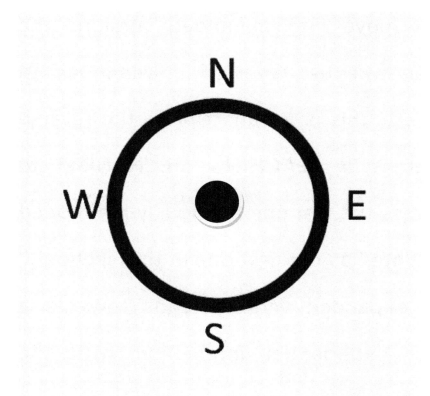

EXPANDED VERSIONS

ROOMS WITHIN THE POLARITIES

As I move into expanded versions the order will be reversed... (reminder to reader – this is a transcript so the reverse order is a **TEACHING MECHANISM** to address the last one previously mentioned presented as the first one in this section).

The expanded version tends towards a more experiential interaction with the material.... To add to the learning process we will change direction and work counterclockwise.

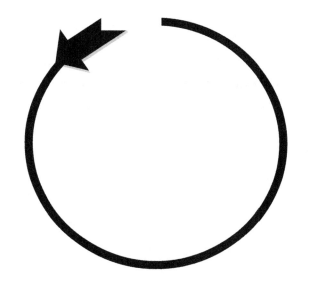

COUNTER CLOCKWISE

WEST

So the first Polarity we are addressing this time is the west.

Just **BE** in the west.... Just **KNOW** what the west does... and in that method of **ALLOWING**, you will experience the west.

If appropriate timing means to you that something has to perhaps have less aggressive movement then you are only looking at one side of the options.

On occasion appropriate timing means that progress must be encouraged by the west – it must push something into quicker action as the delay is the problematic nuance. One could find oneself in the west, and still experience a sensation of stop and go as the west may "decide" that **is** the appropriate timing.

West Polarity South Room - The south will put a greater distance between the process and the target, **moving elements so they are <u>not able to make full contact.</u>** Understand that when you're in the west you're still in the presence of appropriate timing, so adding the southern room of the west to your process will slow it down and **cause broader pauses between action and contact without breaking the overall connection** of the work which you've set into the west. In the west one can set into action a particular practice or ritual resulting in appropriate timing...

Now go ahead and have that experience for about thirty seconds.

Use this box for your initial thoughts....

West Polarity East Room – As the east and the west are on opposite sides and cannot benefit from a split, this is a perfect scenario of why this is useful to discuss that nuance. In the west you are involving yourself in appropriate timing, you're setting into action something that requires appropriate timing, however you feel that you are in a place, or the target is in a place where it appears that appropriate timing could benefit by the assistance of a push. In the eastern room of the west you can adjust that appropriate timing and push it a little bit harder, push it a little bit faster, and change not so much the delivery, rather the **ability** for the individual, (be it yourself or somebody else) to accept what you're pushing towards them.

That is the nuance. You're not just speeding up the activity, you are speeding up the <u>ability to accept the information</u> or experience or outcome or the habitual practice sooner. So now be in the east aspect of the west for about thirty seconds.

Use this box for your initial thoughts....

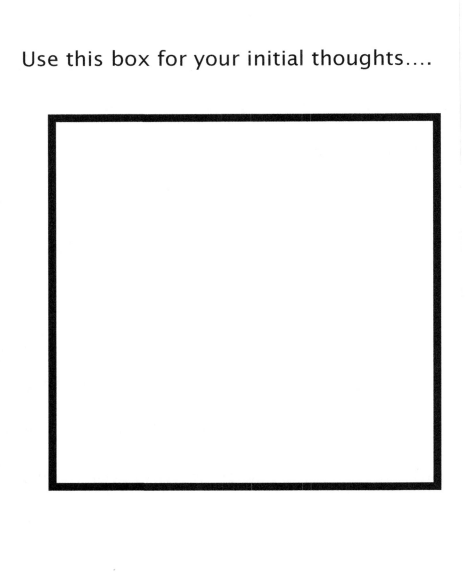

West Polarity North Room – The room in the north will bring to you, a tighter bond, a more powerful connection, so that when the material is delivered it has a higher sticking value. It will stay longer. It will be complete and tidied up in a way that allows for a true finishing with that experience. In the west, you are in the northern aspect of the west, and you are looking for, not changing the timing, but **changing the power of the delivery and of its commitment**.

Therefore, generally speaking, regarding the west, you are in a place of appropriate timing, and the point of this entire exercise is to make clear the purpose of the polarities, and how to use them, consider adding the work of communicating with Daemons. One of the things that could happen in the west is the opportunity to use the north room in this way.

Be in the north room of the west for about thirty seconds.

Use this box for your initial thoughts....

West Polarity West Room – The option that I intentionally do not discuss during the introduction to this class, is that **if you are in the Double Labeled rooms, in this case west and in its own room of the west, <u>you are in pure acceptance of the polarity.</u>** I talked about the word acceptance quite briefly in the past. Here, we are talking about communicating with your Daemons. When you use the western aspect of the western polarity then what you're doing is committing, allowing, accepting the full actions of the west to deliver in appropriate timing, taking out of this equation; your understanding of what appropriate timing might be in this situation.

Allowing for pure physics to make that delivery is extraordinarily useful when doing the kind of work where you have no absolute clarity about how it will be received, and how fast another individual can take in the information. This point of view is also useful when delivering something to yourself, something that is of a heightened emotional level, and you're not sure of the speed in which you can handle the information collected by your activity or the outcome approaching you, post ritual.

So in the western polarity, there is a true western room. I'm going to say just allow yourself to be in that for 30 seconds.

Use this box for your initial thoughts....

SOUTH

So next we're going to address the South.

> Just **BE** in the south.... Just **KNOW** what the south does... and in that method of **ALLOWING**, you will experience the south.

Generally speaking, working in the Static Practice assists one in coming to an understanding of the south. **South is there to break bonds, to push away, to allow and cause release from a circumstance. It's there to <u>lessen a connection, or completely break one</u>.** When you deal with the south and you deal with Daemons, you have to be careful about the directive. When you ask to have someone removed from you, mattering on the ability and the structure of the Daemon, that Daemon might understand that to mean removed from life. You might not mean that. So in that circumstance, these nuances; these inner rooms inside the polarities are quite useful.

South Polarity East Room – We are going to start with looking at the eastern room in the south. This is a highly visceral experience; the eastern room of the south because you are saying that the connection that you desire to break must be broken with immediacy; with top speed, as fast as possible. **This is not the split of the southeast, this is the eastern room in the southern polarity.**

Spend 30 seconds or so taking a look at that.

Use this box for your initial thoughts....

South Polarity North Room – From here we move to the northern room of the south, obviously **they are on opposite sides of the polarity structure, so they have no split.** This is an example of why the rooms are so useful in these previously inaccessible combinations. The northern room in the southern polarity allows you to create sort of a second level scenario where the bond is broken, and the individual with whom it is broken, or the experience with whom it is broken **has the sensation that the breaking has occurred. This is not good when you want to hide something,** but it's very good when you want to say; I have separated from you and **now you feel it too**. The north brings the content of the break straight forward, and still allows for the break to happen. Let me say that again; the northern room in the southern polarity will bring the content of the break forward, making it obvious that this specifically is that from which you broke away.

If what you're breaking away from is a habit, then it allows for the action of the physics to make that thing not be available to you in the way that it has been.

If you want to break away from someone and make sure that the break has happened, and assure that they **cannot cross back over**, the northern room in the southern polarity is where to work from.

This is a serious removal so be <u>quite sure </u>you desire it.

Go ahead and be in that room.

Use this box for your initial thoughts....

South Polarity West Room – The next room in the southern polarity is the western room.

This is a room where malice is part of your intention. Use this room when you are creating a situation where you are separating from something. This is what the south does; for example breaking a bond between the practitioner and the other individual, between the practitioner and a habit, between a client and a habit, or between a client and another individual etc....

The western room will allow for there to be a painful exchange in that separation. It will make the separation just as thorough, but it will be slow and painful and it will be available to be noticed by the target. This is extraordinarily useful if the sensation of malfeasance is part of the reason for doing this separation. That is what happens with the western room in the southern polarity.

Go ahead and have that experience.

Use this box for your initial thoughts....

South Polarity South Room – The final room in the south is the southern polarity in the southern room. The southern room is similar to the western room. **It is an absolute ground zero for the actions of the polarity.** We are all working pretty clearly in the polarities now; we know what they do. Here we are to be in the room of the polarity inside a polarity, the doubly tension if you will. By tension I mean how tightly something is pulled toward the actual polarity.

So what goes on in the southern room of the southern polarity is, **it causes sort of**

a fever pitch of breaking the way one thinks of rubber bands snapping, and buildings falling, and the kind of thing where a breakaway is a powerful, tactile experience, much more so than the western aspect of there being any kind of malfeasance. **I use this when destroying tumors.**

To do so I place the individual, the Practitioner, in the south, and the tumor in the southern room of the southern polarity and they cannot exist in the same place any longer. It sounds very black and white and easy to do, and in some ways it is, and with practice, you can do it yourself. That is what the southern room is for; **it is the absolute ground zero of disconnect.**

Go ahead and have that experience.
Use this box for your initial thoughts....

EAST

Let's move on to the East.

> Just **BE** in the east.... Just **KNOW**
>
> what the east does... and in that
>
> method of **ALLOWING**, you will
>
> experience the east.

The east; speed. Make it happen fast, immediate gratification.

The "I want more"

"I need it faster"

"I want it now"

... and I use **want** and **need** rather than require and desire because it's an ongoing sensation of trying to make things happen faster.

East Polarity North Room - So the first room in the east that we're going to look at is the northern room. **Remember this is not the northeast; it's not the split. It's the northern room in the eastern polarity.** Here we are living in the experience of connections - and **fast** connections. This is an emergency room. **This is the ER of the rooms of the polarities.** If something must happen right away, and that thing that must happen right away has a sensation (this is what the data shows) that it is a thing of super-human capacity:

Examples

*such as getting out of somewhere that causes tremendous danger

*stopping the bleeding of someone who is damaged, and bleeding out

*Holding back a child in utero so that the woman does not lose it early

These kinds of expeditious band-aids on this type of scenario is what the north room in the east is best suited for. I suggest you use it for this caliber of crisis, because **when you start to use it for things of lesser requirement, lesser importance, the careless use of it**

weakens your ongoing ability to grasp that room with the true sense of immediacy,

So go ahead and experience the north room in the eastern polarity.

Use this box for your initial thoughts....

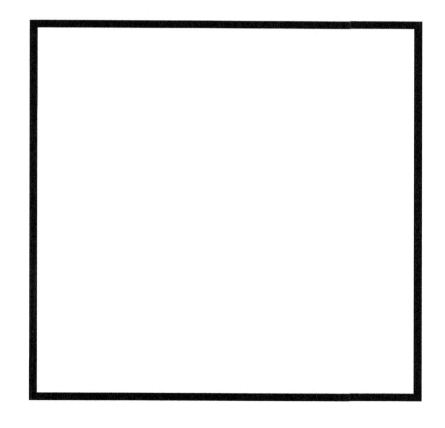

East Polarity West Room – The western room in the eastern polarity is similar in a way to the eastern room in the western polarity, however it has two levels of play, if you will. East makes things happen faster with a focus on forcing things to come to you with immediacy. What the west does is give you appropriate timing. While we talked about it in reverse; the eastern room in the west, there was an understanding about how something comes to you and your ability to receive it.

This is the opposite. Same sensation... opposite side. Consider the image of the yo-yo. The experience of the western room in the eastern polarity is like having the yo-yo on a string. It allows you to pull experiences back and let it go, back and let it go, over and over. **It allows you to utilize a control mechanism. When you let the yo-yo go, the speed is the same as it was before. What the west does is allows you to insert these pauses into the receiving of that which you are creating so that the yo-yo begins to come up, pauses, either goes back down or comes up a bit and pauses etc**...

This can be a torturous experience if what you're creating is a situation where someone is in the desire to receive something with immediacy. It provides the sensation like a stop and go breakup, repeating the difficult moments over and over and over throughout the procedure. Yet once you've pulled the yo-yo back up and you let it flow, it feels like the flow is constant and powerful, going towards the target.

So that is the usefulness of the western room in the eastern polarity. Go ahead and have that experience.

Use this box for your initial thoughts....

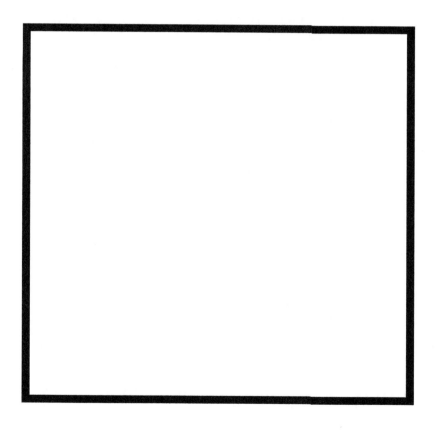

East Polarity South Room – the southern room in the eastern polarity is there to **allow you to control the sensation of reception**. In the east everything moves quickly, in the south things break. **The connection of the southern room in the eastern polarity is to send a sensation of trepidation or of completion.**

One usage is if someone is quite ill, and you've done the work so that they are no longer ill, so that the disease disintegrates, then they will get a sensation of it happening before the cure is set in place in the body.

If you are using the southern room in the eastern polarity to create some devastation on someone or on something, they will find themselves in a state of complete trepidation as if they live in a **constant lingering of knowing it's coming.** Those are the talents of the southern room in the eastern polarity brings.

So go ahead and have that experience.

Use this box for your initial thoughts....

East Polarity East Room– The final room is the eastern room of the east. **It makes something happen so quickly that it distorts time in terms of the receiver.**

If you are working on something where you have a desire to make someone forget something, the eastern room of the eastern polarity is the way to go. What happens here is that **the activity is sped up so quickly that the receiver doesn't perceive it to have happened yet is experiencing the outcome**.... This is a sort of bending of memory.

When you use the eastern room in the eastern polarity, **I strongly suggest that you not use this one upon yourself.** If you want to use this one to release something that has been a burden to you for a great deal of time, I suggest you come to me and ask me to do it. Using the eastern room in the eastern polarity on the self is a double edged sword because **you don't have the recollection that you've done the sorcery, and it causes a modicum of confusion.** so be very careful with this one, and go ahead and experience it.

Use this box for your initial thoughts....

NORTH

The final direction is the North.

Just **BE** in the north.... Just **KNOW** what the north does... and in that method of **ALLOWING**, you will experience the north.

And in any other teaching of the use of Directional Sorcery, I would start with the north and move clockwise from there. This being the advanced group, I have the luxury of going in the other direction. Therefore, let's finish this section by talking about the north, because it's not as obvious as it looks. In the north, things come to you. You go to the north for getting jobs, you go to the north for finding partners, you go to the north for finding new homes, you go into the north for part of the process of fertility, you go to the north to become better at sorcery, or one of the aspects of that. But the north has rooms in it that are quite useful, just as the other three polarities.

NORTH POLARITY WEST ROOM – The first one we are going to look at is the west. The west is appropriate timing, so it has two aspects. When we are looking northwest, and remember this is not a split, it's a room; we have an opportunity to place types of plateaus; areas of leveling off of the delivery of what we're asking to have happen (when I use the word asking, I am not asking for a delivery by any divinity, but rather we are placing this into the work of physics, the way one places a theory or an experience of experiment inside of the process of setting up a ritual for sorcery). The west will stagger the delivery so that it is profound and well absorbed by the target. Of course, one can look at that on two sides; one can say if one is delivering something that has pain or malfeasance, that this creates the ongoing sensation of (ready for this one?) bad luck. **Bad luck is something that isn't real, but it is something to which people who connect each and every uncomfortable thing that happens to them to some sort of connection to the previous**

uncomfortable thing that happened to them are dedicated to manifesting. They create this sensation of a sort of colloquialism labeled bad luck. It can also be used in the exact opposite; west is appropriate timing, north is delivery. You can use it so that yourself or someone else can start to **see opportunity, where no opportunity was able to be seen before.** Somebody who is profoundly pessimistic, somebody who has developed a "belief" of all horrible things in a circumstance where they are unworthy of something. Someone who has accepted a station, if you will, that is less than they think that they are absolutely entitled to or capable of attaining. Using the western room in the north can chip away at that. It can deliver something with appropriate timing, but still at a profound level of delivery. If someone feels that perhaps they not ready, or not worthy of (and I hear that a lot from clients) attaining a new position in the company in which they work, they use this doubt as a failsafe rather than utilizing Sorcery to deliver a promotion to them so that they remain underwhelmed and under challenged. if you use the western room in the north, what happens is that you deliver the responsibilities a little at a time, and then they eventually get the title, via the promotion that goes along with the work which they have learned to do. That's the staggering or plateau-ing effect of the western room in the north.

Go ahead and experience that. Use this box for your initial thoughts....

NORTH POLARITY SOUTH ROOM - The southern room in the northern polarity is **an unfriendly thing to use**, it doesn't mean that you can't use it. It gives the individual upon which you are focused, a sensation that there is always a potential second shoe falling; another thing happening, another rug ready to be pulled out from under them. **You are creating an ongoing trepidation, and this ongoing trepidation of course creates the sensation by the target that they cannot generate personal accomplishment.**

So if you desire to stagger somebody out of something; out of their own opportunity, this is the way to do it.

This is the southern room in the northern polarity.

Use this box for your initial thoughts....

NORTH POLARITY EAST ROOM – the third room; the eastern room in the northern polarity is an opportunity for you to put into somebody else's mind, **that constant sensation of waiting**. Waiting is a very uncomfortable thing. Essentially what I'm saying to you in the eastern room in the northern polarity, you create a sensation of neurosis for someone where they become very high strung, and they are always seeking the next opportunity, almost the way someone seeks out a drug, the next high, or whatever's next all the time, so that they are never living in the moment. It's a pretty nasty device.

Go ahead and experience that.

Use this box for your initial thoughts....

NORTH POLARITY NORTH ROOM – This is sort of the nice guy. This is good delivery, solid information, delivered well, delivered strong, full contact. Don't use it unless there is an agreement of delivery here. Something you absolutely desire, something someone else absolutely desires. Best if all parties are informed. Go ahead and experience that.

Think of this room as the one which delivers well received packages on one's doorstep – however keep in mind that this room controls the delivery – NOT the content of the packages, so be as specific as possible when constructing...

Use this box for your initial thoughts....

I suggest you try these again so that you get the sensations and develop the triggers. For those of you that have them, try some of these in communication with your Attending Daemons and make suggestions or agreements. Set up work that is very clear for them through which the data will prove contact or not. Such as; I haven't heard from someone in a long time and I desire for them to contact me, something that is just straightforward and simple so that you are testing this procedure as well as your ability to follow it in an area in which the data will be clear. Don't start with anything that is yet confrontational or damaging, because if you don't get it right, you might not be damaging enough and poked bears are nasty. So consider that.

This level of the work is, if the reader allows for dramatic language - wizardry. This is used when someone calls me and tells me they are in jam, so I do this, they get un-stuck. This is that kind of thing, so really consider the concept of allow; really look at that, and **see whether you are really <u>allowing allow</u>**, because the sort of inside story of this is that there are rooms in which you can hone up the ability to allow, now that you know that. You can go in there and look at stuff and say; in there is an opportunity to hone that situation up – to allow.

part 2

BLACKHOUSES

BLACKHOUSES

…raw keeps the door open

based on transcripts from

WEDNESDAY NIGHT CORE CLASS

This book not only expands Directional Sorcery to sixteen rooms, it offers the transcripts from classes in which I discuss something about which I have not previously written….

This is dark work....darker than some may find comfortable....

How is it so dark? Well at the front end it appears to be another useful accommodation of the energy and manipulations of the polarities. At the back end of the work, one with a keen eye for nuance will be able to see that this work, the work of the BLACKHOUSES is a way to compile all that has happened to the Practitioner and surrounding circumstances, not store it but rather trap it so that it may writhe in discomfort and become more chaotic, and thereby produce its own amalgam of energies.

This work exposes us…..

I intend to bring the trepidation of the human experience to the table so we can add nuance to the usage of it – not only as a battery and never as a compromise – but rather a method of **trapping the useful debris of experiences**…

To find the right experience to trap, one must work raw. It's hard work to be raw – unfettered by social or cultural restrictions. We are usually unwilling to do so which has nothing to do with laziness…

This work, if fully explored, just taps into the **reverse** of the comfort of not being vulnerable. Yet here's the deal – when working Sorcery - in the true sense of understanding the nuance - **vulnerable** is the only way the shop stays open....

No outcome is guaranteed without putting into place, then acting upon the performance of proactive responses....

There is a cultural mythology in place that all things become even as a matter of fact…. Allow me to present the actuality…

+We don't just get whatever we need

 +We aren't "given" only what we can handle.

+We don't have a capacity to always do everything   for   others.

+We are not guaranteed happiness….

+All things are not busy being equal….

Rather, when it comes to having and fully being, we are obliged to be at war with that which leaves us stranded – alone   and   unfulfilled.....

What do we do with the experiences we can't handle? What do we do with the things that block us – those things that are too hard to negotiate? In a perfect scenario they would surface on the day and time when we are the most capable of handling them, perhaps on a relaxed Tuesday evening when you've had a glass of wine and there is no great challenge – in that moment so you can deal with something that causes upsetment – something that challenges your flow... Perhaps in that moment it doesn't feel like a big deal... It DOES feel like a big deal if it comes up against you when you are dealing with losses or inconsistencies that create the kind of stress the non-Sorcerer still refers to as chaos. Then what do you do when that thing blocks you? **In this class I am going to give you the get out of jail free card. Tonight I will discuss the BLACKHOUSES.**

BLACKHOUSES are not THE BOXES. They are not an effigy – they are not 3D at first – they are tangible, real in the way we have been told to consider reality.....

CONSIDER THIS PROCESS AS IF IT IS AN EQUATION

First you will build them + then you will assign them to the double labeled room + then you fill them, = then you will know that if anything happens to the PHYSICAL BLACKHOUSE, that the double labeled room is the actual location.

CONSIDER THIS....

THE ROOMS ARE IN THE HOUSES – THE HOUSES ARE NOT IN THE ROOMS....

To make BLACKHOUSES work they MUST be something that pushes one's skills, timely to construct and one must feel the grist of the thing. If you were making soufflé for dinner you would make it out of all the required ingredients – build it carefully – watch it cook and handle it all with a certain systematic reverence that is necessary to make important things. You wouldn't try to build it from an instant mix, and if you did you know that it would not be as valuable... BLACKHOUSES require to be physically built first and the actual frustration of building them is the skin of which they are made as that is the very thing that is necessary... It is similar to the thought that in Blood Sorcery – the BLEEDING is not the prized outcome – the interrupting of the vessel and getting closer to death is what is relevant... So the **angst** of construction is the house itself. When it becomes second level tangible – i.e. "as if" virtual – then it will STILL be made from the skin of hard work.

Houses have neighborhoods in which they stand. BLACKHOUSES also have neighborhoods and they are meant to reside in the double labeled rooms. For example, Southern room in the Southern polarity is a neighborhood. Forever keep within the BLACKHOUSES the experiences of your pain, trepidations, misuses, slights, back stabs, dropped balls, when someone has wronged you intentionally – when you have wronged someone intentionally, the fallout from the lover who cheated on you – the hate you feel for someone – the embarrassment of past situations, the doctrine that weighed you down and nearly drowned you, parental influences, bad choices, bad outcomes, addictions, and procrastinations that have caused damage.

Living and working in a place where you are undervalued or where there may be prejudicial actions, deaths you cannot resolve – the ones you can't let go of - these are also things that resolve well and experience a new potential in the BLACKHOUSES.

THERE ARE FOUR PATHS

PATH ONE – BLACKHOUSES are our warehouses for storing what is broken so that those materials DO NOT affect us further.

PATH TWO – BLACKHOUSES are our warehouses for storing these items together. building enough **amalgam chaos** to use as a battery.

PATH THREE – well what else is built from amalgams of chaos? Daemons...

PATH FOUR – CORPORAL NECROMANCY

This book opens up the first two paths, touches on the third, and does not address the fourth path. A book on Corporal Necromancy will eventually be available when I find the time is correct for such a book...

A WORD YOU WILL REQUIRE....

ACREAGE – the action, experience, twinge, - the thing which has affected you and is now being stored.

Let's discuss neighborhoods...

In this section I will repeat the general description of the twice labeled rooms so that the reader has the information all in one place. Then....I will expand the general description into greater specifics regarding the BLACKHOUSES.

EXPANDED GENERAL

DESCRIPTIONS

of the

DOUBLE LABELED ROOMS

WESTERN ROOM OF THE WESTERN POLARITY

In the first class about additional rooms I intentionally did not start with this one. As it pertains to the **BLACKHOUSES** tonight I am going to start here. **Utilizing the BLACKHOUSES delivers, however it is not always comfortable.**

This is dark work. By this I mean that it is visceral, solitary and emotional. In order to do dark work, we must handle dark materials.

To touch into this kind of powerful Sorcery, we have to touch the things that glue us to the memory of lacking. <u>Lacking is a distortion at the source level.</u> The source EXPERIENCE may also be thought of as the ROOT. Therefore, this is the ROOT ROOM. That means that if you are storing something in you **BLACKHOUSES** in this room – it is something that is a PRIMARY DISCOMFORT.

BLACKHOUSES in this room are kicking the foundation of your ugliness – they are built to store the **acreage** that you genuinely feel are ROOT causes. I talked about the word 'acceptance' quite briefly when I first discussed this room - when we were talking about communicating with your Daemons. When you use the Western room in the Western Polarity to store **BLACKHOUSES** then what you're doing is committing, allowing, accepting the full actions of the west to deliver in appropriate timing. You are expecting it to **immediately enact a CECESSATION of the effect of that ROOT ITEM ACREAGE**

to act upon or ever again effect you, taking out of this equation your reaction, your pain and your involvement with that ROOT ITEM ACREAGE from this moment on unless you choose to. Working with ROOT ITEM ACREAGE allows for "pure physics" to fill the void with that which is (as I have been stating and teaching for many years) "heaviest, most familiar and most nearby" as a **delivery function** in the moment the work is done....

Once you have built **BLACKHOUSES** and you read on, you will learn how to hone and use them. Let's discuss what it will look like to INSTALL into the ROOT ROOM, the West Room in the West Polarity that which kicks the foundation of your ugliness. So be "brave" in so much as **you will have to be very honest with yourself.** Consider that this will have pre-emptive effect. If your Root Acreage is causing you to blow up on people when contradicted – that is the CAUSE but not the ROOT. **Remember that we are slicing into nuance here.** Here is a light weight example.

1. Someone is experiencing a sensation of aggravation every time she sees the poster or trailer for that particular film

because she was meant to audition for that film but couldn't get there because the sitter didn't show up. It makes her so angry. So now when she sees those images she immediately feels like something was stolen from her." OK – we are NOT putting the FEELING of something being stolen into the BLACKHOUSE – we ARE putting in the **moment** she realized she were not going to make the audition.

THAT IS FACTUAL SORCERY – PURE, CLEAN AND UN RUFFLED.

NUANCE, for our purpose, is to isolate the tiniest slice which fulfills the requirement.

Let's look at a more intense ROOT ACREAGE EXAMPLE. A man finds that he really hates short blond women. His mother was always **profoundly** verbally and emotionally abusive to him as well as taking his sister's side all the time and treating her as the only important family member. His sister encourages this behavior and mocks him consistently as well. Both his sister and his mother are short blond woman. He fantasizes about killing short blond women. Once night he is in a bar and a short blond woman flirts with him. They go back to his apartment and have sex. So far he is ok, Her phone rings and she says "hang on - it is my mother so you'll have to wait." His fantasies become unhinged as he imagines that she and her mother are mocking him. He flies into a rage and he strangles her. He is convicted of the crime and is in prison for 20 years.

If he were to put the ROOT ACRAEGE of his dilemma into the BLACKHOUSES, he would NOT be putting the strangling or his fantasies into the BLACKHOUSES – he would not be putting his anger in, or the damage done to him – he would be putting his Mother and Sister in the Western Room of the Western Polarity **BLACKHOUSE**.

SETTING UP THE INSTALLATION

Once you have built BLACKHOUSES and you read on, you will learn how to hone and use them. This is what it will look like when you prepare to install the **BLACKHOUSES** and then install within them the Acreage.

I CHOSE TO REPEAT THIS INSTALLATION AFTER EACH BLACKHOUSE SO THAT THE READER WOULD EXPERIENCE THIS LIKE A CLASS AND NOT HAVE TO GO BACK AND FORTH.

IMPORTANT NOTE

BLACKHOUSES hold an infinite amount of Acreage. Use this format to decide what is going in each time you desire to place something into the BLACKHOUSES.

ONLY THE FIRST ONE DEPOSIT OF ACREAGE IN EACH HOUSE REQUIRES THE TRAP TO HONE THE HOUSE. WRITTEN RUN THROUGH

1. Make a choice about what you desire to install. Write the answer here.

2. **Put the HOUSE in the West Room of the Western Polarity.** Do it actually by setting up a diorama of a compass and choose a spot in the West in which to set the BLACKHOUSE. (For those of you who are familiar with this work, also "place" the house in location by energy manipulation and utilizing 3D imaging.)

3. Based on the description of the Western Room of the Western Polarity, choose the aspect of that room which most intrigues

you the one to which you feel the best

connection.   Write your choice here.

4. Have a view of the interior of the house.

In the interior is a trapping device. Think

of the trap as a wild animal trap – glue

trap – mouse trap – anything that allows

for the trapped creature to be seen, so no

quick sand puff mud or bottomless pits.

You will only have to do this once as once

a West in which to set the BLACKHOUSE

has trapped acreage the data shows that all other acreage is simply walked or lured in.

Write details of the trap you envision.

5. Consider the inside of the house, and find a dark corner. You will need to be able to access that dark corner later. Write a note about which dark corner you will use and what it may look like.

6. Have a thought on how you think it will feel and look to trap something in your trap. Write a few words.

NOTE – when you utilize the TIMED INSTILLATION at the end of this chapter, remember that once Acreage is first caught in the trap the house is primed and no other acreage will be able to get out once lured in.

This is very "Dark and intense" work. When you utilize the TIMED INSTILLATION at the end of this chapter, you will see how your movements will apply and you will learn that you never have to enter the house again in order to lure in Acreage. You will learn how to remember the Acreage that is in the BLACKHOUSES

should you desire to use or release it later.

After each time you trap something in a BLACKHOUSES you will be harvesting your Blood then wash it away. Plan to build **BLACKHOUSES** so that you can use the **timed installation** which you will find later in this book. This is extraordinarily useful when doing the kind of work where you have no absolute clarity about how it will be received, and how fast another individual can take in the information. Or, when delivering something to yourself something that is of a heightened emotional level, and you're not sure of the speed in which you can handle the information of your activity or the outcome approaching you, post ritual.

 **NORTHERN ROOM OF THE NORTHERN P OLARITY**

The **NORTHERN ROOM OF THE NORTHERN POLARITY** is the BATTERY PATH ACREAGE of the Black Houses.

Here we store things that are the after effects – the emotional hangovers which we have FELT so we understand how they would feel delivered.

This is the only BLACKHOUSE is which a separate device – AN IRON RING RECALLER is utilized. It allows you to recall the sensation lifted away from yourself – like a remote launching of a firearm. This is sort of the nice guy. This is good delivery, solid information, delivered well, delivered strong, full contact. **Don't use it unless there is an agreement with yourself of delivery here without pause or regret** upon something or someone you absolutely desire to hit **as if** all parties are previously informed. Let's refer to the previous examples. The sensation the person had when they were unable to attend the audition – loss – having something stolen from them - perhaps sabotage? It could be anything that was the emotional hangover – REMEMBER it has to have happened TO YOU and the after effect has to be the smallest most genuine nuance of experience. The man who choked the blond woman – his emotional hangover was not behavioral, it was something more like sadness, abandonment by his mother's choices, mistrust, even self-loathing. I mentioned an IRON RING RECALLER – to be used only in this Black House. To do so place an IRON RING on the emotional hangover and tear it away from the process. Allow yourself to see clearly into the IRON RING and allow ONLY its contents to enter the BLACKHOUSE. Once you have built BLACKHOUSES and you read on, you will learn how to hone and use them. Read on as before in order to experience how that process will serve the practitioner...

I CHOSE TO REPEAT THIS AFTER EACH BLACKHOUSE SO THAT THE READER WOULD EXPERIENCE THIS LIKE A CLASS AND NOT HAVE TO GO BACK AND FORTH.

ALSO - At the end of the chapter is the timed version which one can do and perform the actual instillation.

IMPORTANT NOTE
BLACKHOUSES hold an infinite amount of Acreage. Use this format to decide what is going in each time you desire to place something into the BLACKHOUSES.

ONLY THE FIRST ONE DEPOSIT OF ACREAGE IN EACH HOUSE REQUIRES THE TRAP TO HONE THE HOUSE.
WRITTEN RUN THROUGH

1. Make a choice about what you desire to install. Write the answer here.

2. **Put the HOUSE in the West Room of the Western Polarity**. Do it actually by setting up a diorama of a compass and choose a spot in the West in which to set the BLACKHOUSE. (For those of you who are familiar with this work, also "place" the house in location by energy manipulation and utilizing 3D imaging.)

```
┌─────────────────────────────────┐
│                                 │
│                                 │
│                                 │
│                                 │
│                                 │
└─────────────────────────────────┘
```

3. Based on the description of the Western Room of the Western Polarity, choose the aspect of that room which most intrigues

you the one to which you feel the best

connection.   Write your choice here.

```



```

4. Have a view of the interior of the house.

In the interior is a trapping device. Think

of the trap as a wild animal trap – glue

trap – mouse trap – anything that allows

for the trapped creature to be seen, so no

quick sand puff mud or bottomless pits.

You will only have to do this once as once

a West in which to set the BLACKHOUSE

has trapped acreage the data shows that

all other acreage is simply walked or lured in.

Write details of the trap you envision.

5. Consider the inside of the house, and find a dark corner. You will need to be able to access that dark corner later. Write a note about which dark corner you will use and what it may look like.

6. Have a thought on how you think it will feel and look to trap something in your trap. Write a few words.

NOTE – when you utilize the TIMED INSTILLATION at the end of this chapter, remember that once Acreage is first caught in the trap the house is primed and no other acreage will be able to get out once it has been lured in.

This is very "Dark and intense" work. When you utilize the TIMED INSTALLATION at the end of this chapter, you will see how your movements will apply and you will learn that you never have to enter the house again in order to lure in Acreage. You will learn how to remember the Acreage that is in the BLACKHOUSES

should you desire to use or release it later.

After each time you trap something in a BLACKHOUSES you will be harvesting your Blood then wash it away. Plan to build **BLACKHOUSES** so that you can use the **timed installation** which you will find later in this book. This is extraordinarily useful when doing the kind of work where you have no absolute clarity about how it will be received, and how fast another individual can take in the information. Or, when delivering something to yourself something that is of a heightened emotional level, and you're not sure of the speed in which you can handle the information of your activity or the outcome approaching you, post ritual.

For this house Recall that I said.....
I suggest you utilize this room eventually so that you get the sensations and develop the triggers of the communication with your Attending Daemons when making deals and negotiations which turn into agreements about remote work you desire them to do, both at the recon level and the savage level...

Such as; I haven't heard from someone in a long time and I desire for them to call me, something that is just straightforward simple so that you are testing this recipe, if you will, and your ability to follow it in an area in which the data is clear, and don't do anything that is yet confrontational or damaging, because if you don't get it right, you might not be damaging enough poked bears are nasty. So consider that.

EASTERN ROOM OF THE EASTERN POLARITY

The Eastern Room of the Eastern Polarity is the DESTRUCTION ACREAGE of the Black Houses. **In this BLACKHOUSE we store the sensation of purposeful malfeasance** The final room is the eastern room of the east.

It will make something happen so completely that it distorts time and outcome to the receiver. If you are working on something where you have a desire to break, crumble distort or destroy something, the BLACKHOUSE stored in the eastern room of the eastern polarity is the base reactor storage. What happens here is that the activity is sped up so quickly that the ACTION doesn't perceive itself to have happened. (we will discuss further) This is a sort of bending memory. When you use the eastern room in the eastern polarity,

I strongly suggest that you USE use

this one upon yourself **WHEN SEEKING TO OVERCOME SEEMINGLY INSURMOUNTABLE DISCOMFORT OR ODDS.** If you want to use this one to release something that has been a burden to you for a great deal of time, I WILL TEACH YOU AT SOME POINT to do it. Using the eastern room in the eastern polarity on the self is a double edged sword because **you don't have the recollection that you've done the sorcery, and it causes a DELIGHTFUL CLEAN START**, so be very careful with this one, and go ahead and experience it. This is a personal pain inventory moment.

Malfeasance is best delivered through mimicry and nothing is easier to recollect than when you were in horrific pain. We will not use the same two examples here as there is no way to transfer those particular experiences to the group nor should we. So listen very carefully to the nuance – so look at the moments of devastation that are not logical. If your cat of 25 years becomes ill and dies – this is logical. If your friend has habits that allow for him to be around dangerous people and he gets hurt or killed – this is logical – if you have been a 71% or less participant in a relationship and she sleeps with your boss – logical. However – if you have a full participation and expectation (based on a partner's behavior) that you will get to the wedding and the marriage will happen – and your partner doesn't show up because he has found another lover he prefers – this is illogical.... If your friend who lives a pretty normal life is shot and injured or killed in a drive by – illogical. If you are well and then suddenly diagnosed with a profound un-wellness when you have done none of the life activities that should make such a thing occur – illogical... if your boss chooses someone who is less deserving over you for an important raise or career move – illogical. SO here's the thing – now you have EXAMPLES of illogical – what you don't have is a working equation…a litmus test. The human mind is of course satisfied by equation – so here it is:

I performed in a way that I perceive to be as appropriate + I allowed myself the expectation that this behavior would create a preferred outcome + I am not alone in the world and people make choices and situations have hidden components = an outcome I perceive to be illogical

Remember – the outcome must have plausible upset-ment to qualify as the DESTRUCTION ACREAGE of the BLACKHOUSES. **In this Black House we store the sensation of purposeful malfeasance.** Use this moment as a toxin – a lovely glass bottle full of pain to be poured onto an adversary. .

I CHOSE TO REPEAT THIS AFTER EACH BLACKHOUSE SO THAT THE READER WOULD EXPERIENCE THIS LIKE A CLASS AND NOT HAVE TO GO BACK AND FORTH. ALSO - At the end of the chapter is the timed version which one can do and perform the actual instillation.

IMPORTANT NOTE

BLACKHOUSES hold an infinite amount of Acreage. Use this format to decide what is going in each time you desire to place something into the BLACKHOUSES.

ONLY THE FIRST ONE DEPOSIT OF ACREAGE IN EACH HOUSE REQUIRES THE TRAP TO HONE THE HOUSE.

WRITTEN   RUN   THROUGH

1. Make a choice about what you desire to install.   Write   the   answer   here.

```



```

2. **Put the HOUSE in the West Room of the Western Polarity.** Do it actually by setting up a diorama of a compass and choose a spot in the West in which to set the BLACKHOUSE. (For those of you who

are familiar with this work, also "put" the house there by energy manipulation and utilizing the technique of 3D printing.)

3. Based on the description of the Western Room of the Western Polarity, choose the aspect of that room which most intrigues you the one to which you feel the best connection.   Write your choice here.

4. Have a view of the interior of the house. In the interior is a trapping device. Think

of the trap as a wild animal trap – glue trap – mouse trap – anything that allows for the trapped creature to be seen, no quick sand puff mud or bottomless pits. You will only have to do this once as once a BLACKHOUSE has trapped acreage the data shows that all other acreage is simply walked or lured in.

Write details of the trap you envision.

5. Consider the inside of the house, and find a dark corner. You will need to be able to access that dark corner later. Write a note about which dark corner you will use and what it may look like.

6. Have a thought on how you think it will feel and look to trap something in your trap. Write a few words.

NOTE – when you utilize the TIMED INSTILLATION at the end of this chapter, remember that once Acreage is first caught in the trap the house is primed and no other acreage will be able to get out once it has been lured in.

This is very "Dark and intense" work. When you utilize the TIMED INSTALLATION at the end of this chapter, you will see how your movements will apply and you will learn that you never have to enter the house again in order to lure in Acreage. You will learn how to remember the Acreage that is in the BLACKHOUSES should you desire to use or release it later.

After each time you trap something in a BLACKHOUSES you will be harvesting your Blood then wash it away. Plan to build **BLACKHOUSES** so that you can use the **timed installation** which you will find later in this book. This is extraordinarily useful when doing the kind of work where you have no absolute clarity about how it will be received, and how fast another individual can take in the information. Or, when delivering something to yourself something that is of a heightened emotional level, and you're not sure of the speed in which you can handle the information of your activity or the outcome approaching you, post ritual.

SOUTHERN ROOM OF THE SOUTHERN POLARITY

This is the IMPETUS ROOM – The one that deals with original UNDERSCORING urge and incitement AND IT DOESN'T EVEN HAVE TO BE YOURS. This is THE BLACK HOUSE BATTERY. Black Houses in this neighborhood is another absolute ground zero – however for Battery Work.

Make no error here – it is NOT about root cause – it is about root motivation and THAT is an element of physics we will discuss further next week as it is a DOUBLE TENSION. By tension I mean how tightly something is pulled and delivers not with the sensation of the tautness of a guitar string – but more like the release – the breaking point. **It causes sort of a fever pitch of breaking – a girder snapping buildings falling, an enormous power release...a powerful tactile experience**, much more so than the western aspect of there being any kind of malfeasance.

I use this when destroying tumors. I place the individual, the practitioner in the south, and the tumor in the southern room of the southern polarity and they cannot exist in the same place any longer. It sounds very black and white and easy to do, and in some ways it is, and with practice, you can do it yourself. But that is what the southern room is for; it is the absolute ground zero of disconnect. Absolute ground zero of disconnect. Go ahead and have that experience.

I CHOSE TO REPEAT THIS AFTER EACH BLACKHOUSE SO THAT THE READER WOULD EXPERIENCE THIS LIKE A CLASS AND NOT HAVE TO GO BACK AND FORTH. ALSO - At the end of the chapter is the timed version which one can do and perform the actual instillation.

Important note

BLACKHOUSES hold an infinite amount of Acreage. Use this format to decide what is going in each time you desire to place something into the BLACKHOUSES.

ONLY THE FIRST ONE DEPOSIT OF ACREAGE IN EACH HOUSE REQUIRES THE TRAP TO HONE THE HOUSE.

WRITTEN   RUN   THROUGH

1. Make a choice about what you desire to install. Write the answer here.

2. **Put the HOUSE in the West Room of the Western Polarity.** Do it actually by setting up a diorama of a compass and choose a spot in the West in which to set the BLACKHOUSE. . (For those of you who are familiar with this work, also "put" the house there by energy manipulation and utilizing the technique of 3D printing.)

3. Based on the description of the Western Room of the Western Polarity, choose the aspect of that room which most intrigues you the one to which you feel the best connection.   Write your choice here.

4. Have a view of the interior of the house. In the interior is a trapping device. Think of the trap as a wild animal trap – glue trap – mouse trap – anything that allows for the trapped creature to be seen, so no

quick sand puff mud or bottomless pits. You will only have to do this once as once a West in which to set the BLACKHOUSE has trapped acreage the data shows that all other acreage is simply walked or lured in.

Write details of the trap you envision.

5. Consider the inside of the house, and find a dark corner. You will need to be able to access that dark corner later. Write a note about which dark corner you will use and what it may look like.

6. Have a thought on how you think it will feel and look to trap something in your trap. Write a few words.

NOTE – when you utilize the TIMED INSTALLATION at the end of this chapter, remember that once Acreage is first caught in the trap the house is primed and no other acreage will be able to get out once it has been accurately lured in.

This is very "Dark and intense" work. When you utilize the TIMED INSTALLATION at the end of this chapter, you will see how your movements will apply and you will learn that you never have to enter the house again in order to lure in Acreage. You will learn how to remember the Acreage that is in the BLACKHOUSES

should you desire to use or release it later.

After each time you trap something in a BLACKHOUSES you will be harvesting your Blood then wash it away. Plan to build **BLACKHOUSES** so that you can use the **timed installation** which you will find later in this book.

This is extraordinarily useful when doing the kind of work where you have no absolute clarity about how it will be received, and how fast another individual can take in the information. Or, when delivering something to yourself something that is of a heightened emotional level, and you're not sure of the speed in which you can handle the information of your activity or the outcome approaching you, post ritual.

PUTTING YOUR HAND ON THE BLACKHOUSES

I have offered a template here, just a suggestion, to allow the student to understand that the BLACKHOUSES must first be tangible. I have also added these photos to show how the basic template can lead to self-expression.

IMAGES OF THE SORCERESS'

BLACKHOUSES

BLACKHOUSES TEMPLATE, BASIC STRUCTURE
Copyright SORCERESS CAGLIASTRO

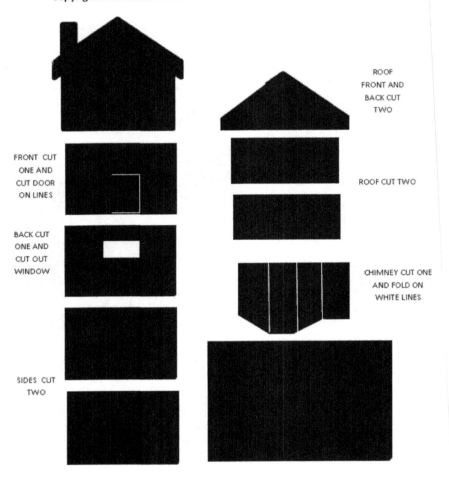

ROOF
FRONT AND
BACK CUT
TWO

FRONT CUT
ONE AND
CUT DOOR
ON LINES

ROOF CUT TWO

BACK CUT
ONE AND
CUT OUT
WINDOW

CHIMNEY CUT ONE
AND FOLD ON
WHITE LINES

SIDES CUT
TWO

BASE CUT ONE

NOTES ON CONSTRUCTION OF THE BLACKHOUSES

The primary concern when building

BLACKHOUSES may seem obvious –

however it is this –

that the BLACKHOUSES must be BLACK.

The data shows that this is the best

format and thusly why they are referred to

as BLACKHOUSES.

I suggest they not be too large, (mine are

only a few inches tall), and they must have

a door which is kept open buy may be

closed if necessary.

They should be black inside and out.

I feel a chimney is lovely however not necessary. I add bases to mine which makes them movable. If you are going to make a diorama, I still suggest you add a base so that the house has a foundation and so that the contents does not touch to "ground" of the neighbourhood.

The houses you see in the images are built from heavy watercolour paper. The pieces are cut with a scalpel and the crisp edges are glued together with super sticky glue. Once the house is dry, it is painted with high quality black craft paint or spray painted.

Paint the inside as well, and if you add a chimney then paint the inside of that also. They must be as black as you can make them. Once you have built the houses, and one should build all four before beginning, consider this check list.

Create a compass board in a safe place so that you may set the BLACKHOUSES down on the board in their exact polarities. Be sure you know the exact location of the polarities. The BLACKHOUSES will be placed in the polarity, then urged into the double-labeled aspect.

1. Do you have a secure place to set them the compass board down so it will not be disturbed?

2. Do you have a device with which to harvest your Blood and a place in which to wash it away?

3. Have you prepared your answers for each of the categories regarding deciding which ACREAGE goes into which BLACKHOUSE for its honing?

Know that when working Sorcery, especially Sorcery that involves such deep self-examination, that things will come up which are unexpected so make sure you have privacy and time to work.

"CLIFF NOTES"

What I refer to as the Cliff
Notes are what follows below
just after the SETUP – FULL
DIORAMA.

It is a set of short reminders of the
definition, purpose and center focuses of
each of the BLACKHOUSES. I have set this
section up so that you can review the
short versions and go right into the
portion that is labeled THE
INSTALLATIONS. Each short review is
followed by a blank page. You can use this

for the first installation in each house.

Going forward you should have a book in which you write everything else you place into the BLACKHOUSES...

PREPARE YOURSELF.....

CLIFF NOTES - WHEN IN IMMEDIACY– IN OTHER WORDS... REPEATED SHORT VERSION OF THE FOUR DOUBLE POLARITIES FOR USE WITH THE BLACKHOUSES.

I chose to repeat these so the reader would experience this part as a class as well. The reader reviews each one then jumps to the times instillation.

NOTE – if you have not taken the classes on BLACKHOUSES, there will be a recording available of this TIMED Installation. It will be available by August 2016. For further information, view the BLACKHOUSES tab on the main site. The tab will go live August 2016 as well.

www.cagliastrotheironring.com

SETUP – FULL DIORAMA

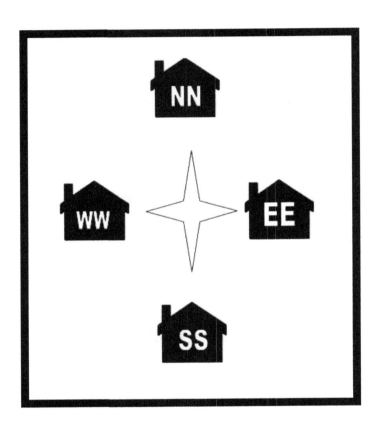

WESTERN ROOM OF THE WESTERN POLARITY

W/W– ROOT ROOM ACREAGE

We have to touch the thing that **glues us to the memory of lacking.** This is the **ROOT ROOM** – So you are storing something in your BLACKHOUSE in this room that is a **PRIMARY DISCOMFORT**.

BLACKHOUSES in this room are kicking the foundation of your ugliness – they are built to store the **ACREAGE** that you genuinely feel are ROOT causes which have left you in discomfort.

 NORTHERN ROOM OF

THE NORTHERN POLARITY

N/N– THE BATTERY PATH ACREAGE

Here we store things that are the **after effects** – the emotional hangovers which we have FELT so we understand how they would feel **delivered**. This is the only BLACKHOUSE which allows for use of a separate device – **AN IRON RING RECALLER** is utilized. It allows you to recall the sensation **lifted away from yourself.**

EASTERN ROOM OF THE EASTERN POLARITY

E/E– THE DESTRUCTION ACREAGE

In this BLACKHOUSE we store the sensation of purposeful malfeasance which has been either perpetrated upon us, or somehow through observation has affected us. Using purposeful malfeasance will **make something happen so completely that it distorts time and outcome to the receiver.**

SOUTHERN ROOM OF THE SOUTHERN POLARITY

S/S–IMPETUS ACREAGE, THE BATTERY

This BLACKHOUSE handles original UNDERSCORING urge and incitement which DOESN'T HAVE TO BE YOURS. This is the BLACKHOUSE ground zero BATTERY. This is NOT about root cause – it is root **motivation**, tense and over-pulled - a principle my students know as DOUBLE TENSION.

PART THREE

THE TIMED INSTALLATION FOR

ALL

BLACKHOUSES

(use individually)

FIRST YOU MUST KNOW THE

POLARITIES, the West, North, East

and South of where you are.

1. Take 2 minutes to make a choice

about what you desire to install –

2. -Take 2 minutes to place the

HOUSE in the (X) polarity of the

(X) room. Do this by physically placing it down (X) of your location. Then "PLACE IT" by allowing it to reside in the (X) polarity of the (X) room

3. Take 2 minutes to consider then pick the aspect of that room that most intrigues you or that you feel the best connection to.

4. Take 3 minutes to 3D print (those new to this work visualize) a Wild animal trap – glue trap – mouse

trap – anything that allows for the trapped creature to be seen, so no quick sand, pluff mud or bottomless pits. You will only have to do this once as once a Black House has trapped acreage the data shows that future acreage is easily lured in.

5. Take 4 minutes to "Go into the house" and place that aspect in as if it is representing the trapping device.

6. Take 2 minutes to look around and move to the back dark corner and Stay in the house while inviting in the acreage. Wait until you feel it is caught in the trap. This may take longer than 2 minutes. You are responding to your sensation of completion.

7. Take 1 minute to prepare to leave the house.

Once the Acreage is caught in the trap the house is primed and no other Acreage will be able to get out once entered.

You will never have to enter the house again – you will know what is inside should you desire to use or release it later. Observe and imprint the appearance of the inside of the **BLACKHOUSE**, then leave. This is very "Dark and intense" work.

8. Take 3 minutes to harvest, anoint the house and wash the Blood away. I strongly suggest that after every time you trap something in a Black House – that you harvest your Blood and wash it away. Do so now. This one time and one time only you may place you Blood on each **BLACKHOUSE.** If you did so by instinct when you made them – then that will do.

DELVING DEEPER INTO THE BLACKHOUSES
(from transcript)

Including NOTES, FAQ's via post class Q&A and email communications.

This class (this is a transcript) will be a further usage of the BLACKHOUSES including questions have been asked by a number of students. I will answer those questions here...

This is one of those nights where the information is intended to bring clarity, however I am fully aware that it may just bring more questions...

The BLACKHOUSES are a new level....

FIRST QUESTION...

1. **Do we need to create a new BLACKHOUSE for each Acreage we are storing?**

POINT A

No, because the data all the way across the board of all of my work shows that there is a certain potential – an "initial energy" in the first presentation into any of the forays into pillars or any other structured significant aspect of the work in general. Therefore, the initial acreage which you chose to trap carries a particular despertism. It goes like this – I am struggling with X – there is a solution available – so I will tap X and use it here – to test the potential solution – to test my skills – fuck it – to get rid of this Acreage. That is the one that is full of angst and has been TRAPPING YOU – which is WHY we use it to be the first trapped and thereby to hone the house.

Point B

Consider this moment – the one which I just described as one that is PERFECT for Mimicry. In moments were the essential energy – the front end energy – the energy required to get out of the chair and push through regardless of the enormity of the wall in front of you caused by the presence of "just Too Much" – use this moment in Mimicry to force through.

POINT C

I said – generally speaking – that additional Acreages are moved into the house by luring and did not mention the trap. I also said that The Trap may be used again if you desire as that which is trapped stays in the house until it is utilized by you. NO one asked how both of these could be true. **The answer anyway is that the TRAP is now transformed by the honing – the TRAP is now your angst – your lack of requirement to manage these Acreages in your daily life ever again. Can you see the nuance there?** However what is meant by Utilize?

There are 2 areas of utilization. First, you can utilize the Acreage as you use that which is in the Static Practice Gallery as you have done by going in and looking and choosing - then utilize that experience in a Sorcery event. The difference is The event – comparing it to acreage - **remains** inside of the Gallery as the Gallery is self-generated. It self – fills, gathering all of your experiences whether you choose to have those materials in it or not. The gallery of the static practice is an inventory of your life. The BLACKHOUSES are not filled that way. They are filled at **your** Discretion and that Acreage can either be used, like the Gallery in the SP, as a touchstone - an "inspiration" for usage in a Sorcery Event **OR** Acreage inside of the BLACKHOUSES can be used as actual ammunition. Using them this way requires sending them somewhere very much as one sends Daemons. In fact – practicing this hones the PRACTITIONER to be able to "send" – and that is where some of you get stuck – on the SENDING of Daemons and so forth.

We have to roll all the way back to the striking of the target. But why would you need to put the item into a BLACKHOUSE to use it this way? Well that is solved

succinctly by remembering that we are not

talking about wishes, pink candles and

flying genies - we are talking about

physics - the innate performance of the

polarities which is heightened by looking

at the rooms within the polarities –

especially the double labeled rooms in

which we place BLACKHOUSES.

> **Once Acreage is in the BLACKHOUSES it is subject to the trial of the energy of that room.**

Example – if you have a thought or sensation that a particular Acreage is a ROOT CAUSE – and you place it in the E/E, then the aspects of the E/E heighten it – grows its "talents" as a root cause if you will, and in that flourishing makes it viral in capacity.

THIS IS WHY YOU ARE PUTTING THESE ACREAGES INTO BLACKHOUSES – THIS IS WHY YOU ARE TRAPPING THEM BECAUSE THEY ARE HEIGHTENED – MADE VITRIOLIC – SO YOU MUST KEEP THEM CONTAINED SO THEY DO NOT HAVE ANY FURTHER ACCESS TO YOU UNTIL YOU CHOOSE TO UTILIZE THEM.

Utilizing them removes them from the BLACKHOUSES, either permanently, indefinitely or temporarily – as prescribed by the Practitioner - and changes their content. I will say that again...

Utilizing them removes them from the BLACKHOUSES, either permanently, indefinitely or temporarily – as prescribed by the Practitioner - and changes their content. The ultimate usage of this is create enough chaos by re-lurking Acreage that has been utilized in Sorcery so that the chaos is profound. What is derived from profound chaos? (food for thought)

SECOND QUESTION

2. Once the Acreage is in the BLACKHOUSES does it relinquish control over us? This question was posed in several different ways by several students. I gathered the questions together to form the succinct question so that I may efficiently respond. I touched on this in the first answer... However, the BLACKHOUSES are not a room – they are a labyrinth – and you will see that as we move forward in this work as you will find that the corner you are hiding in may feel more like another room or another

perspective. They are bottomless...

So for simplicity – if such a thing exists here which it actually does not – so Generally speaking that which goes into BLACKHOUSES is that which has had the most visceral effect on us overall (broadly speaking), therefore, the use of the BLACKHOUSES regarding the nuance of trapping allows us to control the Acreage as opposed to the Acreage controlling us. For example, if one had a sibling who, for endless years, was abusive, one has taken considerable "incoming" (damage) from that situation. Placing the sibling in the

BLACKHOUSES puts the Sorcerer in control of the actions of that sibling going forward - AND thereby, by the act of luring, puts the Sorcerer in control of the previous damage. This is why the BLACKHOUSES are so vitriolic. That being said – two additional forces may be at plat at the Practitioner's hand – once that hand as experience. The Practitioner may choose the action to be **either**

Permanent, Indefinite or Temporary (PIT) which places the Practitioner in the cat position of cat and mouse – which is revenge and well suited for this method.

However – this cat and mouse position allows for continued interaction with the original Acreage – so use the BLACKHOUSE that allows for BATTERY usage (either N/N or S/S depending on the origin of the Acreage) when playing this purposeful game.

To satisfy the human mind by equation I offer the following:

To break it down.....

X says Z hurt him for years + Z is captured by X in the BLACKHOUSES + the BLACKHOUSES are not bound by time = X now has control over the previous damage, the present damage and any future damage intended by Z

Additional equation...

X + BLACKHOUSES trapping Z = Z becomes X's bitch

WEAPONRY

Once one puts Acreage in the BLACKHOUSES - and desires to use that Acreage in Sorcery - how does one get those experiences to be relevant as a weapon or device to use on others....

In other words - how does one turn, for example, a childhood trauma into an arrow...?

I have been very cautious regarding the work imagery... because it has a tendency to be used in glitter and wish-work. For this moment I ask that you suspend the attachment that the word imagery has for use in the language of these materials.

If you have a disorder – arthritis, migraines etc.....and you desire to remove that disorder, then the Science of Sorcery allows for all manner of ways to do so. You can box it and place it elsewhere, you can Bleed it out, Use an Iron Ring to make the boundary between the disorder and you permanent, you can take it from you gallery in the SP and place it elsewhere, you can utilize it in various ways in the 5th pillar giving it new purpose – however all of those options are options that, in most usages, focus on ridding the self of the disorder. Not to say that they are only to be used from that Point of View – however they are more frequently thought of that way. The BLACKHOUSES are a device that operates specifically in a way through the perspective that the Practitioner will be giving that disorder to someone else. This is why I asked you to listen to the word imagery in a different facet tonight.

Examples...If one has arthritis – let's use that – and one has a person in their life who has either been acting in "bad form" for an extensive period of time and/or for a specifically complex malfeasance, then this is a perfect scenario for the **EXCHANGE OF DISORDER.**

EXCHANGE OF DISORDER

Place the Acreage of this situation in the appropriate BLACKHOUSE – in this case the better choices would be NN or SS as they have Battery aspects, and once it is in there – all fighting to get out – make the DEAL THAT IT'S RELEASE IS CONTINGENT UPON RELOCATION. How do we guarantee that? Place a BOX at the door of the BLACKHOUSE that is locked in this moment – and allow the exit of the arthritis to pass through that box only if it is in full compliance – essentially you are utilizing FORCED DIVINATION which is a pre-built forced outcome. See the imagery on the individual with that disorder transferred to them? NO. See the imagery of that person suffering inside of the well dug in disorder. This is, by the way, useful for child abusers and child killers who must be rendered stationary to make it easier for other prisoners to torture and destroy them...

Why not use the BOX and FORCED DIVINATION all the time?

Because not everything requires a concern about releasing the **self** from some disorder or discontent.

How does one get the Acreage out of the house intact and full of purpose?

Acreage can only be released in its full impact, its full character, its full "is" because that is what was placed into the BLACKHOUSE.

There is of course many more options and opportunities with the BLACKHOUSES that I could expand upon (and I will if questions are sent to me), such as:

Once one uses the acreage, what does it become? Can it be used again? Is the Practitioner now free from the Acreage's effects?

These aspects are the baseline for the work itself at the advanced level... If you are not currently studying this work, then consider taking classes, the Beginner Classes will help. If you do not desire to do so, the methods of the work are available in the Blood Sorcery Bible VOL 2 – Striking the Target, and in the Vol 1 of the Science of Sorcery Beginner Course Vol 1. Both are available on amazon at

amazon.com/author/sorceresscagliastro

EXTRA COPY OF COMPASS
FOR PRACTICING PLACEMENT

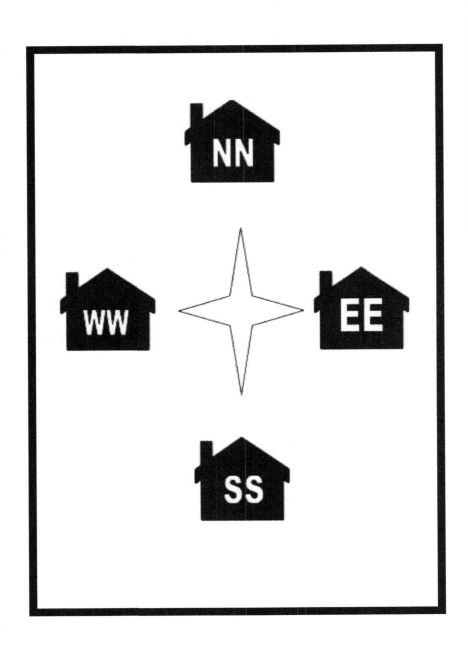

NOTES

WALKING EFFIGIES INTO THE BLACKHOUSES

CLASS transcript

We are now talking about placing effigies into the BLACKHOUSES and utilize that dynamic in both 3d and hand held effigies, as well as using an obtained biological or a personal biological and allowing it to grow into the BLACKHOUSES which is a manner of entity control.

HAND HELD

3D

OBTAINED BIOLOGICALS – Seeds

LURED BLANKS

To build an effigy – especially one meant for the BLACKHOUSES – in this case a 3D effigy you must have these bullets of information

1. Who is this effigy meant to represent?
2. Is the effigy a person or a situation?
3. Is the effigy meant to be volatile?
4. Will the effigy be destroyed in the work?
5. If the effigy is not to be destroyed how is it to be kept?
6. Do I, the practitioner, have malfeasance toward this subject?
7. Does the person who I am representing by this effigy have malfeasance toward the practitioner or the client of the practitioner?
8. Is there a lifelike consideration in this act of Sorcery?

Then consider which CONSTRUCTION method is best based on this assessment. Now we look at the three types that work for BLACKHOUSES

HAND HELD – in this case we must utilize "opticals". Your BLACKHOUSES are small. The same way that building the BLACKHOUSES physically was vital – here it is vital when building hand held effigies that the eye sees them as small enough to fit through the door. When making hand held effigies, remember that the mind which will form the thought to use them, the idea to construct outside value (how to use them) and ultimately the intention of action (which in the Science of Sorcery actually IS action). Therefore, they must fit through the door. Here this is as vital as actually building the BLACKHOUSES as well.

3D - Let's talk about 3D – you know when a 3D construction is completed when you are no longer looking at the development – when you are no longer asking yourself if this looks like that which you are building – but rather you are looking at the item itself – as if it always existed and begin to look at how it fits into the Sorcery event at hand.

OBTAINED BIOLOGICALS – Seeds

Here the Biological is placed within the BLACKHOUSES AND ENCOURAGED TO grow into THE desired EFFIGY. Effigies built in this way become entwined within the BLACKHOUSES and grow into the structure. Very much like in Pirates of the Caribbean – part of the crew – part of the ship. These are unique to the BLACKHOUSES and cannot be separated once they take hold in the structure. They can however become entities – and mimicry of them is suggested. These are most useful as they bring the causation of the requirement of the effigy to begin with into the house.

Let's talk about **3D** – you know when a 3D construction is completed when you are no longer looking at the development – when you are no longer asking yourself if this looks like that which you are building – but rather you are looking at the item itself – as if it always existed and begin to look at how it fits into the Sorcery event at hand.

LURED BLANKS Sending an effigy in is not the same as luring one. A sent in effigy is one that you build (either of three ways) and build it for a purpose. A lured effigy is a blank – and it is lured in to become part of something you have already stored…

Let's do the crossovers….

A hand held is best used as a **sent** effigy – it is sent into the BLACKHOUSE by placing it in feet first and then doing the Sorcery on the experience.

It is also useful at the Divination when attempting to flush out a malevolent individual. Placing its head close to the door and observing over a designated period of time (as open ended periods of time are not methods by which to test your work or gather data) whether it moves closer or further from the door allows one to test someone. For example, if one felt that someone was tapping into an insecurity or weakness of yours by poking at what feels like a root acreage problem then you would utilize the WW room and so forth.

A **3D** effigy can be utilized as sent or lured. As **sent** we create the 3D effigy and place it into the house in order to have it interact with something we have already stored in the BLACKHOUSE.

As lured we place it outside and **CALIBRATE IT** - lay into it a function that is constructed with can and cannot. For example, if (to continue to utilize the same example for continuity) the 3D effigy is part of a root problem it will be lured into the WW as it will exhibit that preset calibration (that being an additional beauty of the 3D effigy). If it is not part of that ROOT problem, it will not "fit" into the BLACKHOUSE

OK so we are going to do four exercises....

WESTERN ROOM OF THE WESTERN POLARITY – root acreage

1. Choose something you keep in this house. You have 2 minutes, then one follow up minute to write your thoughts and experiences.

2. Create a 3D effigy of someone that you feel may be part of this situation You have 3 minutes, then one follow up minute to write your thoughts and experiences.

3. Allow for the luring to occur. You have 2 minutes, then one follow up minute to write your thoughts and experiences.

NORTHERN ROOM OF THE NORTHERN POLARITY – battery path

1.Choose something you keep in this house. You have 2 minutes, then one follow up minute to write your thoughts and experiences.

2.Create a 3D effigy of someone that you feel may be part of this situation. You have 3 minutes, then one follow up minute to write your thoughts and experiences

3. Allow for the luring to occur. You have 2 minutes, then follow up minute to write your thoughts and experiences.

EASTERN ROOM OF THE EASTERN POLARITY- destruction acreage

1. Choose something you keep in this house. You have 3 minutes, then one follow up minute to write your thoughts and experiences.

2. Create a 3D effigy of someone that you feel may be part of this situation You have 3 minutes, then one follow up minute to write your thoughts and experiences

2. Allow for the luring to occur. You have 2 minutes, then one follow up minute to write your thoughts and experiences.

SOUTHERN ROOM OF THE SOUTHERN POLARITY – impetus room

1. Choose something you keep in this house. You have 2 minutes, then one follow up minute to write your thoughts and experiences.

2. Create a 3D effigy of someone that you feel may be part of this situation You have 3 minutes, then one follow up minute to write your thoughts and experiences.

3. Allow for the luring to occur. You have 2 minutes, then one follow up minute to write your thoughts and experiences.

Where are most likely things that surprise you when looking through your answers... and those things are situations which will best be served by placing them into the BLACKHOUSE under which they were revealed in the exercises... that is the purpose of accommodating this new information...

EXTRA COPY OF BLACKHOUSE TEMPLATE

BLACKHOUSES TEMPLATE, BASIC STRUCTURE
Copyright SORCERESS CAGLIASTRO

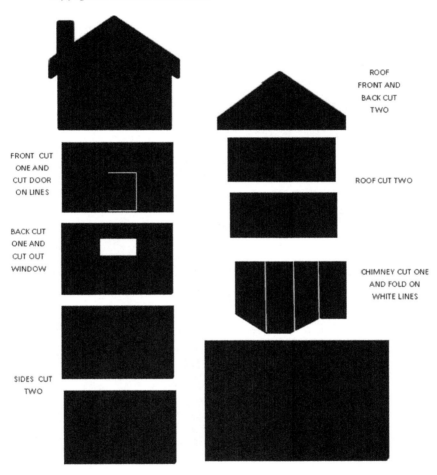

ROOF
FRONT AND
BACK CUT
TWO

FRONT CUT
ONE AND
CUT DOOR
ON LINES

ROOF CUT TWO

BACK CUT
ONE AND
CUT OUT
WINDOW

CHIMNEY CUT ONE
AND FOLD ON
WHITE LINES

SIDES CUT
TWO

BASE CUT ONE

NOTES

NOTES

BIO AND BOOK CATALOG

**SORCERESS CAGLIASTRO,
BLOOD SORCERESS, NECROMANCER IN THE HANDS
OF 9....**

... author, publisher, lecturer, teacher, Daemon Handler,

Necromancer, and Exorcist, creator of THE IRON RING, a Science of Sorcery practice through which to explore the broader gaze of the experience of Sorcery. It was created for and is taught to individuals of a mindset to learn Blood Sorcery, Necromancy, Divination, Directional Sorcery, The Static Practice, other Pillars and the broad gaze of the work. The Sorceress is a lifelong practitioner of and the foremost authority on Science of Sorcery, Blood Sorcery and the related Pillars of the Iron Ring Method…

The Sorceress has authored the Blood Sorcery Bibles Vol 1 and Vol 2 and many other books on the Science of Sorcery as well as fiction and screenplays based on her experiences with Daemons and the Disincarnate. Recently, through her publishing company North Sea Tales, the Sorceress has also published books under the project name of "Rescued Knowledge Project, A Cagliastro Endeavor". These are historical books of a broad gaze of interests. They are available in paperback and a few of them are currently available on the Kindle. All of her books are available on Amazon, keywords Sorceress Cagliastro or visit her amazon author page at amazon.com/author/sorceresscagliastro.

Classes with the Sorceress are available on live via live stream - however seating is limited, as her classes and teaching are very popular both in the United States and Internationally. Starting this year, she is offering "Learn As You Go", giving Beginner Students the chance to study and learn Blood Sorcery and the Science of Sorcery through the Pillars. That thorough six-month class offering, is taken on your time via recorded sessions, and students have the opportunity to meet individually on live feed (on line) with The Sorceress monthly as part of the program.

FOR FURTHER INFORMATION - OR FOR PRESS INQUIRIES

sorceresscagliastro@gmail.com

THE SORCERESS CAGLIASTRO,

Blood Sorceress, Necromancer in the hands of 9

For more information about The Science of Sorcery or to study with The Sorceress Cagliastro visit **www.cagliastrotheironring.com** or Email sorceresscagliastro@gmail.com

BOOKS BY
THE SORCERESS CAGLIASTRO

TITLES BY THE SORCERESS CAGLIASTRO CAN BE FOUND AT
amazon.com/author/sorceresscagliastro

*THE SCIENCE OF SORCERY BEGINNER COURSE VOL 1
(NECESSARY FOR BEGINNERS)

*BLOOD SORCERY BIBLE VOL 2 – STRIKING THE TARGET
THE PRACTITIONER AND THE STATIC PRACTICE (BEST
IN THE SERIES)

*26 DAEMONS REVISITED

* MENSTRUAL BLOOD AND SEMEN – A SORCERY
MANUAL

*BLOOD SORCERY BIBLE VOL 1 – RITUALS IN
NECROMANCY

*BLOOD SORCERY BIBLE VOL 1 WORKBOOK

*DIVINATION – THE PRACTITIONER'S MANUAL

*23 SIGILS OF SELFISH INDULGENCE

*25 SIGILS, DARK CIRCLES FROM THE IRON RING

"29 DEADLY SIGILS FROM THE BOY"

*FLATLINE RITUAL, VENGEANCE THROUGH DREAM
INTERRUPTION

*PROTECTION CLASS

also by Sorceress Cagliastro…

*LEONA RETURNED – SCRIPT

*MINI STORIES OF JUSTICE: 7 REALLY SCARY TALES AND
LOTS OF UNDESERVED CONSEQUENCES

*"…and then Minami's baby died…" ORIGINAL BOOK

*"…and then Minami's baby died…" SCRIPT

*DOUBLE CROSSED - Script

UPCOMING NOVEL
**Collette Mandolino Begins to Cry expected
September 2016**

BLACK HOUSES ARE OCCASIONALLY
AVAILABLE ON THE MAIN SITE. THEY ARE USEFUL AS
THEY HAVE BEEN ON THE AUTHOR'S ALTAR. ONE
WOULD BENEFIT FROM HAVING THEM, AND YET
WOULD STILL BENEFIT GREATLY FROM MAKING
ONE'S OWN BLACKHOUSES.

www.cagliastrotheironring.com

CONTACT INFORMATION

For author information or for submission guidelines
for North Sea Tales please visit
www.northseatales.com or contact
northseatales440@gmail.com

For your Sorcery Requirements,
Readings/Consultations, to become a
student of the Science of Sorcery, or for information
about THE FIRM...

sorceresscagliastro@gmail.com

BLANK PAGE FOR NOTES

BLANK PAGE FOR NOTES

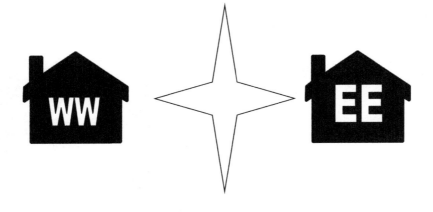

www.cagliastrotheironring.com

Printed in Great Britain
by Amazon

37138850R00175